GIVE US
THIS DAY
A 365-DAY DEVOTIONAL

GIVE US
THIS DAY

A 365-DAY DEVOTIONAL

HERBERT
LOCKYER

W

WHITAKER
HOUSE

All Scripture quotations are taken from the King James Version of the Holy Bible. Scripture quotations marked (asv) are taken from the American Standard Edition of the Revised Version of the Holy Bible.

Give Us This Day:
Daily Portions for Pilgrims

ISBN: 978-1-62911-563-4
eBook ISBN: 978-1-62911-585-6
Printed in the United States of America
© 2015 by Ardis A. Lockyer

Whitaker House
1030 Hunt Valley Circle
New Kensington, PA 15068
www.whitakerhouse.com

Library of Congress Cataloging-in-Publication Data (Pending)

1 2 3 4 5 6 7 8 9 10 11 **W** 22 21 20 19 18 17 16 15

PREFACE

While this is another book of daily meditations, it will be found different from all others, in that an effort has been made to unify themes. In the compilation of these readings, the somewhat busy pastor was kept in mind. Collating seven verses or so around one given theme would, I felt, provide a fitting topic for a prayer meeting message or Sunday morning sermon, thereby making one's preaching consecutive and doctrinal. The author hopes that he has presented a volume that will be of practical worth, as well as of devotional value.

—*Herbert Lockyer*
Liverpool, England

FIRST WEEK

GOD OUR FATHER

JANUARY 1

In the beginning God...
—Genesis 1:1

God has stamped His name and sovereignty upon the very forehead of His Book. God first! This is surely the keynote of the initial book of the Bible. God is first in everything—in creation, in redemption, in providence, in personal experience.

May we take such a majestic utterance as our motto as we face another year with all its hidden cares, trials, and responsibilities! God first in all things will bring us a life in which all its needs will have immediate, divine attention.

JANUARY 2

Thou God seest me.
—Genesis 16:13

Omniscience produces comfort for the saint, but conviction for the sinner. The latter tries to hide from God's all-seeing eye, while the Christian rejoices that such an eye is upon the righteous. What a joy it is to know that His eye is upon the sparrow and that He watches me! Here I am, a nonentity, a mere nobody, yet I am never out of God's sight. May we ever strive to live the life, bringing pleasure to Him whose care of us is personal and intimate!

JANUARY 3

A God ready to pardon.
—Nehemiah 9:17

The beauty of this glimpse of the divine character is not that we have a pardoning God, but that He stands with a pardon in His hand, so to speak, waiting for the sinner to accept it. This God of great kindness need not be coaxed into pronouncing the criminal forever cleared from guilt. He is *ready* to pardon. Yes, and let it be noted that this completed, offered pardon was made possible by the ruby blood of the Son of Him who freely offers such a gift.

JANUARY 4

We ought to obey God rather than men.
—Acts 5:29

Vast hordes of people, robbed of personal freedom, are forcibly obedient to cruel leaders. Our obedience, however, is one of love. Sometimes the question arises, "Can we obey God and man at the same time?" The answer is, "Only when the commands of men harmonize with those of God." When there is conflict between the two, then obedience to God comes first, as brave Pastor Niemoeller is proving in his horrible confinement. Whom do you obey?

JANUARY 5

The God of patience and consolation.
—Romans 15:5

Patience and consolation! What a pair of graces! Patience is the grace to wait—consolation, the grace of waiting victoriously, conscious that what patience waits for will be possessed. Eternal patience is God's. Man occasions Him multiplied disappointments, but tirelessly

He waits for the consummation of His redemptive plan. And as He waits, He is consoled by the ultimate goal of complete sovereignty. Do you need patience and consolation? Then take them as gifts from Him who is their source.

JANUARY 6

God was manifest in the flesh.
—1 Timothy 3:16

A God in flesh! Such was the miracle and mystery of the incarnation. But when God became man, a unique creation was made possible, for the Holy Spirit fused deity and humanity together, producing thereby the God-man. The Spirit became the love-knot of the two natures.

Is God continuing to manifest Himself in your flesh? Is your body "a mysterious cabinet of the Trinity," as Jeremy Taylor expresses it?

JANUARY 7

God is faithful.
—1 Corinthians 1:9

Like a golden thread, the faithfulness of God runs through the Scriptures. No wonder Jeremiah cried, *"Great is thy faithfulness"* (Lamentations 3:23). We are so fickle, spasmodic, disloyal, but there is never a flicker in the lamp of divine faithfulness. There are times, too, when friends prove to be unfaithful. Amid wrecked friendships, however, we can be sure of God. Let us, then, feed on His faithfulness.

SECOND WEEK

THE LORD JESUS CHRIST

JANUARY 8

Where Christ should be born.
—Matthew 2:4

While Christ as a "child" was born in Bethlehem, as Micah had predicted, yet as the "Son," He was from everlasting. Strange though it may seem, then, Christ lived before He was born. And this is one of the glories of the gospel. The Ancient of Days *became* a babe. He who is without beginning and without ending condescended to indwell a body prepared for Him. The practical thought, however, is evident. Christ's birth in Bethlehem will avail nothing, unless He is born within your heart and mine.

JANUARY 9

The devils [demons] knew that he was Christ.
—Luke 4:41

Whatever the demons may be, they are certainly not among the modernists who deny the deity and authority of Christ. Hell assents to His claims as the anointed of God. Had He been a man, merely, power would never have been His to rebuke the emissaries of Satan. They recognized in "Christ, the Son of God" as the demons called Him, One greater than themselves and even greater than the devil, their prince. How wonderful our Christ is!

JANUARY 10

Ought not Christ to have suffered.
—Luke 24:26

No, in one sense, He should not have suffered. Even the dying thieves confessed that their royal companion in anguish had done nothing amiss. Why should the holy One take away our sins? Why should the Innocent suffer for the guilty?

Well, blessed be His name, He willingly endured the cross as our Sin-bearer. He bore the accursed load, and now there is none for me. But suffering grief, He earned the right to enter glory. Grief and glory are strange companions, yet the one is the steppingstone to the other.

JANUARY 11

Christ was raised up from the dead.
—Romans 6:4

Some of the old divines spoke of the resurrection as "God's receipt for Calvary." Yes, we know the debt of sin has been cancelled for Jesus rose again. The empty grave made possible our justification.

But the apostle Paul, ever gifted at giving doctrine a practical turn, associates the resurrection of Christ with the believer who must endeavor to walk in newness of life. Have you had your resurrection? Do you daily arise from your dead self to a higher life in Christ?

JANUARY 12

Christ sitteth on the right hand of God.
—Colossians 3:1

The epistle to the Hebrews reminds us that it was after the grim work of Calvary that Christ sat down on the right hand of the Majesty on high. The sitting posture, therefore, is indicative of a completed task. It is also suggestive of a privileged position as the result of conquest. And that we share the exaltation of Christ is evident by the fact that we have been made to sit together with Him. (See Ephesians 1:20; 2:6.)

JANUARY 13

Christ, who is our life, shall appear.
—Colossians 3:4

Presently appearing in the presence of God for us, the unseen Christ is to manifest Himself even as Joseph revealed himself to his brethren. His dazzling glory, radiant beauty and perfect power will captivate us and swell our praises. What is beyond our human comprehension is the thought that we, presently despised because of our allegiance to Him, are to appear with Him in glory. Then we shall be like Him in every degree.

JANUARY 14

We are made partakers of Christ.
—Hebrews 3:14

There is, of course, a difference between *take* and *partake*. "Taking" means "to accept" while "partaking" implies "having a share in." Well, as we *take* Christ as our personal Savior, we are made *partakers* of all that He is and has. Accepting Christ, He immediately assures us that all that He has is ours. Here, then, is the only "sharing" the Christian rejoices in. Are you claiming your share?

THIRD WEEK

THE HOLY SPIRIT

JANUARY 15

…the holy Spirit of God.
—Ephesians 4:30

Over one hundred times the Bible reminds us of the Spirit's inherent holiness. And He is well-named *"holy"* seeing that He comes from a holy God, magnifies a holy Son, and strives to fashion us unto love and all the holiness within the Trinity. Yes, and being holy, the gracious Spirit cannot countenance anything within your life and mine contrary to His holy mind and will.

JANUARY 16

Where the Spirit of the Lord is, there is liberty.
—2 Corinthians 3:17

Rotherham, in his *Emphasized New Testament,* translates this Pauline phrase thus: "Where the Spirit is Lord, there is liberty." What do we know about the lordship of the Spirit? When He is Lord, then there is liberty in prayer, in witness, in worship, in giving, in service. A believer in bondage is one who fails to recognize the Spirit's lordship. Are you rejoicing in the liberty of His presidency, as well as in the fact of His presence?

JANUARY 17

The Spirit of God descending like a dove.
—Matthew 3:16

The symbol of the dove illustrates the nature of the Spirit Himself and of His ministry. The dove is the love-bird. It is said that it is a bird without any gall. We hear sermons on "The love of God" but never any on "The love of the Spirit." But that He is the Spirit of love is proven by the fact that He can be grieved. Grief is a feeling of the heart. Our possession by the Spirit of Love means the exhibition of a loving spirit.

JANUARY 18

Sensual, having not the Spirit.
—Jude 19

The twofold significance of the term *"sensual"* is given as "depending on the senses only," and "self-indulgent or licentious." The narrative would suggest the usage of the latter interpretation of the word. The last time is to witness a terrible manifestation of animal passions and licentious pleasures, Jude declares. Yet, taking the finer word, is it not likewise true that these are days of religious exercises appealing to the sense only? Some churches are sensuous, fascinating the esthetic in man. The Spirit, however, is missing. Are you sensuous or spiritual?

JANUARY 19

The Spirit also helpeth our infirmities.
—Romans 8:26

The particular "infirmity" the Holy Spirit assists us in is our inability to pray as we ought. Being within us He understands our human needs and emotions, and as a part of the Trinity He likewise knows the mind of God and can therefore make intercession according to the divine will.

There is, however, a larger application of the Spirit's ministry as a "helper." No matter what our infirmities may be, we have in the Spirit of power an unfailing source of strength and succor.

JANUARY 20

Quench not the Spirit.
—1 Thessalonians 5:19

The word *"quench"* carries with it the idea of "putting out the fire." Fire, as we know, is one of the symbols used to describe the Spirit's ministry. If the Lord's, then the Holy Spirit is our "eternal inhabitant" as Saint Augustine called Him. Therefore, quenching Him does not mean putting Him out of the life, but the smothering or damping of His operations. And, as Paul emphasizes, this can be done by our adverse criticism of those who are trying their best to witness for Christ.

JANUARY 21

The fruit of the Spirit.
—Galatians 5:22

A cluster of nine graces compose the Spirit's fruit. The first three are related to our inner life—the next triad to our outer life—the last trinity of virtues to our life godward. And the believer cannot produce the fruit by self-effort. The Holy Spirit *produces* it. The child of God simply *bears* it. *"From me is thy fruit found"* (Hosea 14:8). Further, much fruit is not the outcome of much work. Professed results are not necessarily the fruit of the Spirit. They may only be the product of the energy of the flesh.

FOURTH WEEK

THE ANGELS OF GOD

JANUARY 22

Joy in the presence of the angels of God.
—Luke 15:10

Sinners repenting occasion the angels' great rejoicing. They share the joy of the Shepherd Himself as lost sheep are found. Christ did not die for angels, yet nothing thrills them like the sight of sinners turning to the Savior. Are we contributing to the joy of angels and to the satisfaction of Christ? We were wont to sing in gospel meetings, "There are angels hovering round to carry the tidings home." Alas, the majority of churches, destitute of soul-saving activities, send the angels away with sad hearts.

JANUARY 23

The angels of God met him.
—Genesis 32:1

"God's host," (Genesis 32:2) Jacob called the angelic company meeting him on his way to the old home. Fear of Esau was dispelled by the sight of the divine protectors and companions. If you are called upon to tread perilous roads, face arduous duties and endure grievous trials, go your way and the angels will meet you. There are those who believe that every Christian has a guardian angel. Glory may reveal how much we truly owe to the emissaries of heaven.

JANUARY 24

Four angels standing on the four corners of the earth.
—Revelation 7:1

The varied ministry of these legions of God is one of the most fascinating themes of Scripture. Here they are found exercising relegated power over material forces. Holding in check mighty winds blowing from every quarter, the angels preserve the earth from disaster. The thought, however, we take for our hearts is this—It does not matter in what corner of the earth we may be or where our loved ones live, threatened dangers are ever under control of angelic protectors.

JANUARY 25

Angels came and ministered unto him.
—Matthew 4:11

Twice over, after grim contests, angels hastened to Christ with their ministry of consolation. The wilderness and Gethsemane encounters left Him physically exhausted. Yet a mystery of our faith is the fact that although Jesus was higher than angels, in His humanity He evidently needed their beneficent aid. Just what heavenly cordials they administered to the needy Christ we are not told. It is apparent, however, that soothed and strengthened by their attention, the Master faced further sorrows with a fresh determination.

JANUARY 26

…for they are equal unto the angels.
—Luke 20:36

Some of us can still remember how as children, we used to sing with great gusto, "I want to be an angel, and with the angels stand." Well, the fact remains that we shall never be angels nor have wings. Ours is to be a more exalted and privileged relationship. Why, we are to judge angels! When our Lord spoke of equality with angels He referred, of course, to their deathless and sexless nature. Angels adore the Lord—let us equal them here, nay, surpass their praises, seeing He shed His blood for us and not for angels.

JANUARY 27

His angels he charged with folly.
—Job 4:18

Angels can sin, Peter reminds us. And although they were angels God did not spare them. Justly He charged them with their folly. If angelic beings are capable of prostituting their lofty privileges and position, how great is our peril, seeing we have not the environment angels are used to. And yet we are encouraged even by the judgment of angels for such is an evidence of a divine holiness that must be recognized and exhibited.

JANUARY 28

Nor angels...shall be able to separate us from the love of God.
—Romans 8:38–39

That angels have enormous, relegated power is seen in the work of the angel who smote 185,000 Assyrians. Peter speaks of angels as being *"greater in power and might"* (2 Peter 2:11) than proud, evil men. Yet so indissoluble is the bond between Christ and His own that an archangel or angel is not able to break it. In Christ we are eternally secure. No force, heavenly, human, or hellish can divide the Savior and the saved. Hallelujah!

FIFTH WEEK

SIN

JANUARY 29

By one man sin entered into the world.
—Romans 5:12

Here is a tragic illustration of Solomon's dictum about one sinner destroying much good. All the tears, sorrow and losses grave sin has caused can be traced back to the one sin, one man committed. Through the obedience and sacrifice of another Man, however, myriads of souls have been and are being blessed. And because influence is never neutral, each of us is helping others heavenward or hellward. Is your life a blessing or blight?

JANUARY 30

Fools make a mock at sin.
—Proverbs 14:9

Only a fool could be guilty of such mockery. But belittle a sin as he may, it ever arises to mock the fool who likewise cries, "There is no God!" Mocking or minimizing sin does not do away with it however. Satan has some people deluded into believing he does not exist. Well, if there is no devil, we want to know who is carrying on his business. In like manner, if sin is only human frailty, or the just expression of human nature, then it is a very sordid and destructive force. Sin is sin, and must be hated. Its wages is death.

JANUARY 31

Christ died for our sins.
—1 Corinthians 15:3

What a mystery! He who knew no sin was made sin—not a sinner—for us. Was made sin! Who can fathom the depth of this startling statement? The sinless One made sin? Yes, it pleased God to make His Son an offering for sin. And as He died, it was as the sinless Substitute of sinners.

> There was no other good enough
> To pay the price of sin;
> He only could unlock the gate
> Of Heaven, and let us in.
> (lyrics from "There is a Green Hill Far Away")

The question is: has Jesus, Who died for your sin, become your personal Savior?

FEBRUARY 1

The blood of Jesus Christ his Son cleanseth us from all sin.
—1 John 1:7

All sin! What a gospel to preach! And, truly, "*all*" means ALL. When Satan troubled Martin Luther about his past sins, the monk urged the devil to catalogue them all, and this done, he challenged the tormentor to write over the ugly list that the blood had cleansed him from all his sins. But why has the blood such efficacy? It is because in some mysterious fashion it carried the fusion of deity and humanity. The blood of a mere man, however good, could never atone for sin.

FEBRUARY 2

Sin shall not have dominion over you.
—Romans 6:14

God has left no place in His program for sinning saints. There is no reason why they should sin. The Holy Spirit is within that they might not sin. If they do sin, Christ pleads His efficacious blood before the Father's face. Are we dead to sin? Remember, sin does not die, but we have grace to die to sin. Sin is not to reign over our mortal body. And the only way by which sin can be constantly dethroned is by the constant enthronement of Him who is stronger than Satan and sin.

FEBRUARY 3

Be sure your sin will find you out.
—Numbers 32:23

Scripture, history and experience testify to the fact that sin is a master detective. Moses knew what he was writing about, for the detection of his slaughter of the Egyptian meant forty year of solitude. Man may try to hide his sin and the effects of it but at last it tracks him down. Ultimately he sows what he reaps. He can never sin in the dark as far as God is concerned. If exposure does not come in time there is always eternity to reckon with.

FEBRUARY 4

Whatsoever is not of faith is sin.
—Romans 14:23

Doubt concerning certain habits and pleasures can be taken as a sign that we are not to engage in them. A safe principle is: When in doubt, don't! If we are convicted that a habit, say smoking, is not right for us as Christians to practice, then if we continue the habit, it becomes a sin. Is something troubling you which somehow does not fit in with your Christian witness? Then give the Lord the benefit of the doubt and quit whatsoever is not of faith, lest continuance, with the light you have, becomes sin.

SIXTH WEEK

DEATH

FEBRUARY 5

By one man sin entered into the world, and death by sin.
—Romans 5:12

While Adam, the federal head of the human race, brought sin and death because of sin, into the world, Paul makes it clear that every grave is the result of personal sin. Death passed unto all men, for that all sinned. The soul that sinneth, *it* shall die. Thus all the tears, separations, heartaches and graves death produces can be traced back to the source of sin. Had there been no sin, one wonders what would have happened to souls with no death to take them from the earth. Possibly like Enoch we would have been translated as wanted in heaven.

FEBRUARY 6

Deliver them who through fear of death
were all their lifetime subject to bondage.
—Hebrews 2:15

How many there are who all their lifetime are subject to bondage. And that such a fear is instilled by the devil, who before Calvary had the power of death, is evident from the narrative. Well might many around tremble at the thought of the grave. They are not saved. Sin has not been dealt with. And, oh, the terribleness of dying without Christ! To those unprepared for eternity, death comes as a brutal foe. But to those who are the Lord's, death approaches as a beneficent friend. And why should we fear such a friend ushering us into the glorious presence of our adorable Lord?

FEBRUARY 7

Let me die the death of the righteous.
—Numbers 23:10

May our last end be like the triumphant departure of those who look on death as a transition! It is said that John Wesley was proud of his preachers seeing that they could die well. The victorious death of the righteous is precious in the sight of the Lord. Job speaks of those who die in full strength being wholly at ease and quiet. D. L. Moody's death utterance is memorable, "This is glorious. Earth receding, heaven is approaching. God is calling." God grant us a similar end!

FEBRUARY 8

There is but a step beneath me and death.
—1 Samuel 20:3

Seeing that our breath is in our nostrils we do not know when it may please the Lord to withdraw it. You may be nearer heaven than you think. Today you may take the step leading from one boundary to another. Death, of course, can reach us in many ways, naturally or tragically. Without a moment's warning the summons may come. Well, if it does, to the child of God, sudden death is sudden glory. The moment we are absent from the body we find ourselves at home with the Lord.

FEBRUARY 9

She that liveth in pleasure is dead while she liveth.
—1 Timothy 5:6

Dead and alive! What a contradiction of terms! Yet such is a true description of multitudes who have a name and are physically alive, but are dead. Much animation is theirs in worldly matters. They are alive physically, mentally and socially, but dead spiritually. In physical death the spirit is separated from God. Jude mentions those who are *"twice dead,"* (Jude 1:12) that is, dead spiritually, dead eternally. Pleasure lovers, dead to God, await the second death.

FEBRUARY 10

We are buried with him by baptism into death.
—Romans 6:4

Mystic phrases such as *"dead...unto sin"* (verse 11), *"dead with Christ"* (verse 8), *"mortify the deeds of the body"* (Romans 8:13), *"baptism into death,"* are all related to the death-life of the believer. The power of a resurrected life can never be ours unless we have a grave. And the reckoning of ourselves dead indeed to sin and self is a daily death. With Paul, we must die daily. Dr. Alexander Maclaren has it, "The life of self is death: the death of self is life. Which life is yours?"

FEBRUARY 11

The dead in Christ shall rise first.
—1 Thessalonians 4:16

Not all the dead are to rise at Christ's return, only the dead in Christ. The rest of the dead, the wicked dead, must remain in their graves until the great white throne. When Jesus comes, then the saint will be able to shout, *"Death is swallowed up in victory. O death, where is thy sting?"* (1 Corinthians 15:54–55). Now death is an enemy, but with the last enemy it will be destroyed for us at the Second Advent. What a blessed hope!

SEVENTH WEEK

JUDGMENT

FEBRUARY 12

Now is the judgment of this world.
—John 12:31

For the believer, there is no condemnation, seeing sin was judged and forever dealt with in Christ, when He was lifted up from the earth at Calvary. Being justified by His blood, we shall be saved from wrath through Him. The Law pronounced a curse upon disobedience and demanded death as a penalty. At the cross, Jesus Christ bore the curse and suffered the penalty. "He bore the accursed load and now there's none for me." And, blessed be His name, He will not demand another payment.

FEBRUARY 13

If we would judge ourselves...
—1 Corinthians 11:31

The chastening self-judgment produces is not to be confused with condemnation. In Christ Jesus we have no condemnation, for He bore and banished it. Chastening, standing for genuine repentance over unworthy ways and a fuller, more complete surrender to the Lord, is ever the fruit of an honest judgment of self. Plato declared that the unexamined life was not worth having. Do you ever sit in judgment on yourself? It is easy to judge our neighbors, and harshly. Self-judgment is usually more merciful.

FEBRUARY 14

We must all appear before the judgment seat of Christ.
—2 Corinthians 5:10

Nothing can revolutionize life and service like the constant thought of this judgment for believers only. Service and not sins form the issue of every man's *work* and is to be tried by fire. And *loss*, if service is not up to the divine standard, is the loss of reward. Such a judgment is to determine our place and position in coming glory. May we be spared the sorrow of having a saved soul but lost life when the record is unfolded! Let us go in for the highest reward.

FEBRUARY 15

Before him shall be gathered all nations: and he shall separate them.
—Matthew 25:32

The dramatic judgment outlined in the narrative concerns the nations of the earth when the Son of Man comes in His glory. Three classes are found at this vast tribunal—sheep, goats, and brethren. By "my brethren" we can understand the Jewish people, while the sheep are the Gentile nations, kind and beneficent in their treatment of the Jew. The goats are the other nations, cruel and stubborn in their approach to the Jews. And it is not hard to separate the nations now. Democracies harbor the Jew—dictatorships persecute him.

FEBRUARY 16

I will cause you to pass under the rod...I will purge out from among you the rebels.
—Ezekiel 20:37–38

The terse comment of one writer reads, "The passage is a prophecy of the future judgment upon Israel, regathered from all nations into the old wilderness of the wanderings. The issue of this judgment determines who of Israel in that day shall enter the land for kingdom blessing. And what a sifting there will be when the Lord pleads with His ancient people face to face. Rebels there will be unfit for kingdom responsibilities. They can be found now in those Jews irreligious and sordid."

FEBRUARY 17

The angels…reserved in everlasting chains under darkness
unto judgment of the great day.
—Jude 6

The judgment of the fallen angels vitally concerns the believer seeing that he is to assist the Lord in such. "*We shall judge angels*" (1 Corinthians 6:3). It would seem as if these former occupants and servants of heaven will be arraigned at the same time as Satan, the one responsible for their fall. Do you ever wonder what share we are to have it this pathetic scene? It would seem as if there is a connection between this judgment and self-judgment. If we are easy and tolerant with ourselves, how can we be qualified to judge angels? In another connection, Paul speaks about judging others and yet excusing ourselves.

FEBRUARY 18

A great white throne…and the dead were judged.
—Revelation 20:11–12

What a dreadful judgment the final one will be! Thank God, if we are at the judgment seat of Christ we will not experience the horrors of the great white throne. Here all the wicked dead, raised from earth, sea, and hell, are made to stand before the august Judge to receive the ratification of their condemnation. What hopelessness and eternal despair clothe the scene! And yet what final triumphs of the conquering Christ it presents. Death and hell are cast into the lake of fire! All foes are subjugated.

EIGHTH WEEK

ETERNITY

FEBRUARY 19

He hath set eternity in their heart.
—Ecclesiastes 3:11 ASV

Within the breast of both saint and savage can be found the hope of immortality. Men may try to deny the existence of an after-life, but ever and anon, the God-implanted desire for continuance beyond the grave expresses itself. The old-time question *"If a man die, shall he live again"* (Job 14:14) is answered by intuition and revelation. Our hearts and the Bible declare the fact of immortality. Death, then, is not the end of all, but simply an episode.

FEBRUARY 20

The high and lofty One that inhabiteth eternity...
—Isaiah 57:15

Reading the verse as a whole the prophet Isaiah makes it clear that God has two homes. People of affluence boast two abodes—a town house and a country house. Well, God inhabits eternity, yet condescends to live within the contrite and humble heart. And there is no reason to dread eternity, a high and holy place, where God dwells. Thinking of ourselves as the home of the high and lofty One, we have need to pray, "O make my heart Thy dwelling place, and worthy of Thee."

FEBRUARY 21

...who through the eternal Spirit offered himself without spot to God.
—Hebrews 9:14

Eternity is one of the transcendent attributes of Deity. As Christians, we are the recipients of eternal life. We do not, however, possess eternity. We are to live forever, but we have not lived from the countless ages of the past. Pentecost witnessed the coming of the Holy Spirit from heaven as the gift of God, but He existed before Pentecost, just as Jesus lived before He was born. And, is it not blessed to realize that the same Spirit, bequeathed to us as a guide and comforter, is not to vanish at our death? He, too, as the eternal One, will follow us into eternity.

FEBRUARY 22

...suffering the vengeance of eternal fire.
—Jude 7

Beloved, we fail in our sacred mission if we hesitate to warn the unsaved to flee from the wrath to come. Hell, the present abode of lost souls, and the lake of fire, their future and eternal environment, are grim realities. Magnifying the love of God, man may try to quench the fires of retribution but on they burn. No one personified the love of God as Jesus did, yet He stands out as the greatest preacher of hell the world has ever had. It was He who spoke of it as the place where the worm never dies, and the fire is never quenched.

FEBRUARY 23

From everlasting to everlasting, thou art God.
—Psalm 90:2

As the Lord, He is without change or variableness. Do you ever pause to praise God for His changelessness? What a terrible lot ours would be if we had a God who was subject to the whims and fancies causing men to be so unreliable. What God has been, He will be! He is the same yesterday, today, and forever.

And Moses, in his prayer, reminds us that time cannot affect divine sovereignty. Ancient thrones may crumble, but from eternity to eternity, God is ever God. Satan and men may try to dislodge Him, yet how futile their efforts. In a changing world, then, let us cling to the changelessness of God.

FEBRUARY 24

The eternal God is thy refuge,
and underneath are the everlasting arms.
—Deuteronomy 33:27

What a beautiful and comforting sight this is into the divine character! If you are cast down by the sorrows and cares of life, the unfailing arms are ever beneath to support and succor. *"Who is this that cometh up from the wilderness, leaning upon her beloved?"* (Song of Solomon 8:5). Are we leaning all our weight upon the everlasting arms? Bishop Heber has a precious verse we should have near at hand in the dark hours of life,

> There is an Eye that never sleeps
> Beneath the wing of night;
> There is an Ear that never shuts
> When sink the beams of light;
> There is an Arm that never tires,
> When human strength gives way;
> There is a Love that never fails,
> When earthly loves decay.

FEBRUARY 25

...everlasting life.
—John 3:16

Everlasting life is equivalent to Jesus Christ. Everlasting life is *"life eternal"* (John 17:3) and the Master is the eternal One. This is life eternal and this is in His Son and is His Son. Yet the full complement of the eternal life which commences at regeneration is future. Ultimately it will mean the full enjoyment of the Savior's presence and the full employment of all our glorified faculties in His blessed service.

NINTH WEEK

GRACE

FEBRUARY 26

The God of all grace.
—1 Peter 5:10

Grace, which has been called "unmerited favor," had its rise in the heart of God. Marvelous, is it not, that the One sinned against made possible the salvation the sinner needed? The hand torn by man's sin, offers mercy far and wide.

And, although God can never excuse our iniquity, yet as the God of grace, He deals kindly with the repentant. Let us hasten to tell sinners, then, that the God they must deal with is not a tyrant or despot, but One whose grace is abundant.

FEBRUARY 27

The grace of God was upon him.
—Luke 2:40

Grace, then, is not some*thing* but some*one*. God did not send grace to man, it was brought in the person of His beloved Son. "*Grace and truth came by Jesus Christ*" (John 1:17). And in all His works, words, and ways, He manifested the grace of God. Grace was poured into His lips and emanated from His life. And when, ultimately, He died as the Innocent for the guilty, the true nature of grace was revealed. Jesus died that we might live. Amazing grace!

FEBRUARY 28

Grace did much more abound.
—Romans 5:20

Sin reigned! Grace reigns! What a contrast of sovereigns Paul presents in this chapter exalting the gift of grace! Abounding grace, however, making possible our liberty, does not mean license. There is a false doctrine abroad, asserting that when saved you can do as you like. But surely matchless grace demands that we must live as He likes. We must not presume upon grace. Shall we sin that grace may abound? God forbid. When grace reigns, all other claimants for the throne of the heart are deposed.

MARCH 1

Singing with grace in your hearts to the Lord.
—Colossians 3:16

Here is a challenging motto to hang in the choir room of a church! Strict attention to this Pauline exhortation would revolutionize any choir, which Charles H. Spurgeon called "the war department of the church." A singer has no right to sing spiritual songs unless he or she has the grace of God in the heart, enabling them to sing not merely for show or for the praise of men, but as unto the Lord. Have you the gift of song? If so, do you employ your gift from right motives? Mark the two requisites of effective singing—grace in the heart—unto the Lord.

MARCH 2

The grace of the fashion of it perisheth.
—James 1:11

Grace, as used by James, implies charm, loveliness, and attractiveness of nature. And how heat, drought, and storm can ruin such! Yes, and a good deal of the grace and culture wealth makes possible likewise fades away, as James goes on to say. But the grace of God and the graciousness it produces are indestructible. If saved by grace, no one and nothing can rob us of such a gift.

MARCH 3

*Grow in grace, and in the knowledge of
our Lord and Saviour Jesus Christ.*
—2 Peter 3:18

It will be noticed that we do not grow *into* grace but *in* it. No person can grow into salvation. Regeneration is a crisis. Once within the sphere of grace we grow within it, just as the child begins to grow once it is within the world. Grace, as Dr. C. I. Scofield points out, is associated with service, Christian growth, and giving. What progress are we making in these directions? Are we growing? As in nature, so in grace, dwarfs are a monstrosity.

MARCH 4

…as good stewards of the manifold grace of God.
—1 Peter 4:10

Grace imputed and imparted must become grace communicated. Receiving the gift we should transmit it. But what exactly is this manifold grace we are to bear to others? Is the grace of God as exhibited in the death of His Son, for a few elect souls, or is it for all men? Well, take the word *grace* and strike out the "G" and you are left with *race*. Grace, then, is for the race. And we are only faithful stewards as we go into all the world proclaiming the grace of the Lord Jesus Christ, who, by His poverty, enriches all who turn to Him.

TENTH WEEK

ATONEMENT

MARCH 5

...by whom we have now received the atonement.
—Romans 5:11

Paul's statement indicates the fact that Christ both supplies and applies atonement. God has nothing to offer apart from His Son. Our Lord's own Word is very emphatic on this point—*"But by me"* (John 14:6). Christ, then, is the Mediator and Medium. By atonement we are to understand reconciliation. Through Christ man is reconciled to God. God has never had any need of being reconciled to man. Sin brought estrangement from God. The cross brings us back again into fellowship.

MARCH 6

Wherewith shall I make the atonement, that ye may bless the inheritance of the LORD?
—2 Samuel 21:3

What would you say is the greatest blessing flowing from the atonement? All blessings, of course, are now ours in virtue of Calvary. We are blessed with all spiritual blessings in Christ. The principal boon atonement bestows is deliverance from the penalty and guilt of sin. The word *atone*, when divided, spells "at one." Christ, then, by His death, causes the believing sinner to be at one with God.

At peace with God! How great the blessing
In fellowship with Him to be,
And from all stains of sin set free,
How rich am I such wealth possessing.
(lyrics from "At Peace with God! How Great the Blessing")

MARCH 7

Jewels of gold…to make atonement for our souls.
—Numbers 31:50

As the Old Testament word for *"atonement"* conveys the idea of something being covered, the Israelite was allowed to appease God in various ways. Here, for example, the spoil of Midian was presented to the Lord to make atonement for the soul. Under grace, however, acceptance with God cannot be bought. Alas, there are those who try to buy their way into God's favor but it cannot be done. All the jewels in the world could not purchase salvation for a conscience-stricken soul. We must come as beggars and without money and without price, accept God's gift. Once saved, we can surrender all the jewels of gold the Savior's cause should have.

MARCH 8

Make an atonement for them:
for there is wrath gone out from the Lord.
—Numbers 16:46

Sin occasioned the anger of God. Calvary made possible the appeasement of divine wrath. The believer is no longer under wrath, present or future. What we sometimes forget, however, is the solemn truth that the sinner is still under condemnation. *"God is angry with the wicked* [sinner] *every day"* (Psalm 7:11). *"He that believeth not…the wrath of God abideth on him"* (John 3:36). Our pressing message, then, as we face lost souls, is *"Kiss the Son, lest he be angry"* (Psalm 2:12).

MARCH 9

Do no work…it is a day of atonement.
—Leviticus 23:28

God cannot save man on a fifty-fifty basis, partly grace, partly self-effort. When Jesus cried, *"It is finished"* (John 19:30), He had before Him man's complete deliverance from sin. Yet there are deluded souls who think that God must have a little assistance in the salvation so sorely needed. By self-righteousness, good works, and even religion, earnest hearts endeavor to help God. "Do not work…it is the day of grace."

No merit of thine own
Upon His altar place;
All is of Christ alone,
And of His perfect grace.
(lyrics from "At Peace with God! How Great the Blessing")

MARCH 10

An atonement for himself, and for his household.
—Leviticus 16:17

Under the Jewish economy, household atonement played a prominent part in the ritual of the tabernacle. Ere leaving Egypt the blood had to be sprinkled upon the portal of the house, carrying thereby deliverance from death for all within the blood-sprinkled house.

MARCH 11

Atonement money…for the service of tabernacle.
—Exodus 30:16

God has ever been particular about the kind of money used in His service. The gold of the godless carries no value in the treasury of heaven.

And, let it be said, the work of the Lord can get on very well indeed without the money of the unconverted. God's work, when done in God's way for God's glory, never lacks the divine supply. Blood money, that is, the substance of blood-washed men and women, is of great assistance in the spread of the gospel. Do you realize that Calvary has a definite claim upon all that you *have* and *are*?

> Take my silver and my gold,
> Not a mite would I withhold.
> (lyric from "Take My Life and Let It Be")

ELEVENTH WEEK

JUSTIFICATION

MARCH 12

How then can man be justified with God?
—Job 25:4

Job's question finds an answer in Paul's declaration that God is *"just and the justifier of him which believeth in Jesus"* (Romans 3:26). Just and yet Justifier! How is God able to clear the guilty sinner upon whom He had pronounced death? Condemned yet pardoned. Believing in Jesus supplies the answer. He died in the sinner's room and stead. True to His justice, God had to punish sin, which He did in Christ. Appropriating the Sin-bearer, the believing sinner is forever cleared from the Law's just verdict.

MARCH 13

If I justify myself...
—Job 9:20

From Adam down, man has endeavored to justify himself. Plausible arguments excusing sin have been easy to find. But can *"a man full of talk be justified?"* (Job 11:2). Elihu was angry with Job, seeing that *"he justified himself rather than God"* (Job 32:2). Jesus had it against the Pharisees that they justified themselves. (See Luke 16:15.) But in spite of all his self-justification, man stands condemned in the sight of a thrice-holy God. *"In thy sight shall no man living be justified"* (Psalm 143:2).

MARCH 14

Being justified freely by his grace.
—Romans 3:24

To be justified freely not only means that Christ's redemptive work provides a full complete justification from the just claims of the Law, but that the most unworthy can participate in such a provision. Paul speaks about the free gift, but are not all gifts free? Nothing can be a gift if we have to pay for it. The value of our gifts, however, is determined by the love we bear to those about to receive our gifts. Merit, then, prompts and guides our giving. To give to an enemy would be a "free gift," that is, without any cause or merit. Such is the giving of God. Although His enemies and altogether without human merit, He justifies us.

MARCH 15

Justified by faith.
—Romans 5:1

The apostle Paul has been rightly called "the Apostle of Faith." Everywhere in his epistles, especially in Romans, he emphasizes the truth that faith, and faith alone, actualizes what Christ made possible by His death and resurrection. Light in the room where these lines are being written, is possible for electricity is running through the wires, and lamps are waiting to give an unseen power expression. But ere the possible can be made actual, I must put my finger on the switch producing, thereby, the contact between the possible and the actual. Faith, Paul tells us, is the switch.

MARCH 16

Justified by his blood.
—Romans 5:9

Raised again for our justification.
—Romans 4:25

We link these two together for the simple reason that the death and resurrection of Christ form the basis of our justification. When presenting the gospel to sinners we must be careful never to disassociate the death of our Lord from His resurrection. To say that we are justified by His blood is true, but only half a truth. Had Christ remained in the grave there would have been no salvation. But now, believing in his heart that God raised Christ from the dead, the sinner can be saved. (See Romans 10:9.)

MARCH 17

Whom he justified, them he also glorified.
—Romans 8:30

To be justified means to be brought up before God as if we had never sinned. And what a miracle of grace this is! Yet such is the scope of redemption that our future is covered and assured. Love is to perfect what it begins. Having begun a good work of justification, the Lord is to carry it on to our glorification. Positionally we are with Him already in glory. The realization of our transformation into the likeness of the Justifier, however, will come to us at death.

MARCH 18

Justified by works.
—James 2:21, 25

There is no contradiction here of Paul's doctrine of justification by faith. James the Just was a very practical man, who believed in outward signs of inward grace. "*For as the body without the spirit is dead, so faith without works is dead also*" (James 2:26). Both Abraham and Rahab were justified by their works, that is, what they did was an evidence of what they believed. We cannot work for our justification, but by the life we live after we are justified we can demonstrate our heavenly position. Justified, we must be just at all times and in all things.

TWELFTH WEEK

PEACE

MARCH 19

The God of peace shall bruise Satan under your feet shortly.
—Romans 16:20

Some six times in the New Testament we have the designation, *"The God of peace."* And to take this distinguishing feature, noting its connections, would make a very profitable Bible reading. God, not only bestows peace, He is Peace. Peace is not only one of His attributes, it is a part of His nature. And as the God of peace, everything antagonistic to His peaceful nature must be destroyed. It is comforting to know that Satan, as the god of unrest and disorder, is to be dealt with finally. At Calvary the Prince of Peace dealt him his death blow.

MARCH 20

Acquaint now thyself with him, and be at peace.
—Job 22:21

It is surely wrong to urge a sinner to make his peace with God. Peace was secured at the cross, and is now offered as a gift. Therefore all that one with a troubled conscience can do is acquaint himself with Him who is our Peace, and as Job reminds us, when we are at peace with God, *"good shall come unto thee"* (verse 21).

My friend, are you acquainted with God? If not, why not end all your unrest and conflict of soul by the acceptance of a blood-purchased peace?

MARCH 21

The meek...shall delight themselves in the abundance of peace.
—Psalm 37:11

Perhaps you have heard of the old woman whose life had been a constant struggle against poverty. She had never seen the sea. On being shown a vast expanse of water for the first time she exclaimed. "Thank God there's something there's enough of!" Well, there is enough of peace. God always supplies more than enough. Millions have drunk from the river of peace, and yet there is room for millions more to stoop and drink and live. The provisions of the gospel are exhaustless. Truly, the well is *deep!*

MARCH 22

He is our peace.
—Ephesians 2:14

Peace, then, is not something, but Someone. Peace is a Person. "To make Himself... peace." Paul, of course, here states the mystery of the gospel, namely, the reconciliation of Jew and Gentile into one body. All enmity between the two has been done away by the cross. The middle wall of partition has been broken down. Both the privileged and underprivileged can share in the provision of grace, seeing that peace is preached to them afar off and to them that are nigh.

MARCH 23

There is no peace, saith the LORD, unto the wicked.
—Isaiah 48:22

The prophet gives us a graphic description of the turmoil and conflict raging within the breast of the godless. "*The wicked are like the troubled sea, when it cannot rest, whose waters cast up mire and dirt*" (Isaiah 57:20).

And how unsettled the sinner is! A craving for satisfaction creates a ceaseless round of worldly pursuits and pleasure. He seeks peace, but finds it not. Sometimes death is sought in order to end unsatisfied yearnings for peace. Suicide, however only plunges the wicked into the fierce restlessness of hell.

MARCH 24

On earth peace.
—Luke 2:14

In a war torn world, the Christmas carol of the angels sees a contradiction. Pacifists cried, "Peace, peace," but nations have been destroyed and millions upon millions of souls beggars as the result of a world-wide conflagration. And what else do we expect save the wholesale destruction of countless thousands seeing that Satan is the god of the world? As a murderer from the beginning, he is responsible for the river of blood flow over the earth. Over nineteen hundred years ago the Prince of Peace was crucified and the world has been stained by human blood ever since. But peace will yet reign on earth. Christ is coming to fashion a warring earth into a paradise.

MARCH 25

Peace I leave with you.
—John 14:27

Christ was so poor, He had nothing to leave. He needed to make a will. And yet the greatest bequest ever bequeathed was the peace Jesus here calls *"my peace."* Think of His calm unruffled spirit amid the turbulent forces surrounding Him! He could sleep in a wave tossed boat with a storm raging. No wonder He said that the world had no peace to give comparable to His own peace, and such a legacy is for every child of His. Have you staked your claim?

THIRTEENTH WEEK

OUR LORD'S INCARNATION

MARCH 26

How can he be clean that is born of a woman?
—Job 25:4

One of the mysteries of our Lord's birth is that He was born of a woman, and of a woman who recognized her need of a Savior for her spirit rejoiced in God, her Savior, yet He was clean. How, then are we to account for the clean coming out of the unclean? Within the womb of Mary, the Holy Spirit laid hold of that part of the Virgin's birth out of which our Lord's body was to be formed, and He purified it, as the alchemist purifies his metal.

MARCH 27

Mary…was found with child of the Holy Ghost.
—Matthew 1:18

That Jesus had a human mother but not a human father is the evident truth of Scripture. He is the only babe without a father the world has ever known. Our Lord was conceived of the Holy Spirit and born of the Virgin Mary. And John makes it clear that we are not true believers unless we accept the fact that Jesus was born of God. If we try to explain the incarnation, we lose our reason; if we deny the incarnation, we lose our soul. Without the incarnation, the entire fabric of Christianity totters to the ground.

MARCH 28

He that is born King of the Jews.
—Matthew 2:2

Born King! This is truly a striking phrase. One of royal blood can be born a prince, but can only become a king on the death of his father or queenly mother as the case may be. But Jesus was *born* a King. An indirect evidence, surely, of His pre-existence. He was born a King seeing that He was a King before His birth. Paul called Him *"the King eternal"* and *"the blessed and only Potentate, the King of kings, and Lord of lords, who only hath immortality"* (1 Timothy 1:17; 6:15–16). It is interesting to notice that in writing of the Savior, Matthew uses the capital "K" but in describing King Herod, he gives him a small "k."

MARCH 29

Born this day...a Saviour.
—Luke 2:11

Jesus, the name given to our Lord by the angel before His birth, means *"the salvation of God"* (Luke 3:6). Strange though it may seem, Jesus was born that He might die. We are born to live. Christ, however, entered the world in order that He might die as the Savior of men. Virtually slain in the past eternity, He assumed a human body that the salvation conceived in the heart of God might be completed. Jesus came not to present Himself as a model of our obedience, or as an exemplar, but to save us from our sins. Rejecting His Saviorhood, we miss the sole purpose of the incarnation.

MARCH 30

Unto us a child is born, unto us a son is given.
—Isaiah 9:6

The miracle of the incarnation was the fusion of deity and humanity within the body of Mary. Thus, as a child, Jesus was born; but as a Son, He was given. The Child of Mary, the Son of God, and our Lord appeared, then, not as God exclusively but as the unique combination we call "The God-Man." As the Man Christ Jesus, He understands our human needs, and as God He can meet every one of them.

> I hold His hand as on we walk
> And still He holdeth mine;
> It is a human hand I hold,
> It is a hand Divine.
> (Horatius Bonar, *Until the Day Break*,
> "I Know Whom I Have Believed)

MARCH 31

God sent forth his Son…to redeem.
—Galatians 4:4–5

Agreeing with Paul, John reminds us that Christ was manifesto that He might destroy (or undo) the works of the devil. Bethlehem and Calvary are thus united. The one was the step to the other. Have you ever noticed that the denial of the Virgin birth carries with it the denial of the redemptive purpose of the cross? The modernist, rejecting the incarnation, has little to say about Christ dying for sin, and the works of the devil, the virgin birth and redemption by blood stand or fall together.

APRIL 1

To this end Christ both died, and rose, and revived, that he might be Lord both of the dead and living.
—Romans 14:9

What is the use of Easter gatherings and exercises if they do not result in deeper sanctification of life, and in a more resolute endeavor to crown Jesus Lord over all? Good Friday and Easter Sunday proclaim the kindred truths of Saviorhood and Sovereignty. Jesus died that He might become my Savior, and rose again that as the living One, He might be supreme in my life, as a redeemed child of His. Have you given Jesus His coronation? Willingly He endured the dark horror of Calvary and went down to the grave, conquering death, that lordship might be His. Will you gladden His heart at this season by crowning Him King?

FOURTEENTH WEEK

OUR LORD'S SINLESSNESS

APRIL 2

That holy thing which shall be born of thee
shall be called the Son of God.
—Luke 1:35

By *"that holy thing"* we are to understand the body of Jesus. Man is born in sin. Christ, by the Holy Spirit, was born holy. Bringing with Him His own unsinning nature as God, there was added to it an unsinning body. Because of His holy conception, Christ did not enter the world with evil propensities. We are born with a bias in the wrong direction, but with Christ it was different. Apart, then, from the work of the Spirit, we cannot account for the sinlessness of Jesus.

APRIL 3

Which of you convinceth me of sin?
—John 8:46

Our Lord could make this confession of sinlessness without assumption. Unflecked holiness was His. Spotless purity characterized His life and ways. The ministry of the Spirit is to convict of sin, but He could find no fault in our Lord. Thus God and man testified to His sinless character. Had He committed only one small sin, He would have forfeited the right to die as the sinless Substitute for sinners. It is our Lord's sinlessness that gives His blood such abiding efficacy.

APRIL 4

I find no fault in this man.
—Luke 23:4

Pilate, persuaded that Christ was not guilty of any foul deed, declared three times over that He was without fault. Trying to rid himself of the responsibility of having delivered Jesus over to the Jews for crucifixion, he dramatically declared that he was innocent of the blood of such a just person. Disturbed dreams forced Pilate's wife to add her confession to that of her husband regarding Christ's faultlessness. She urged Pilate to have nothing to do with such a just Man. Herod, likewise, could find nothing worthy of death in Him. And His companions in anguish and shame testified that while they were suffering the due reward of their deeds, Christ had done nothing amiss.

APRIL 5

He hath made him to be sin for us, who knew no sin.
—2 Corinthians 5:21

It will be noticed that Christ was *made sin,* but not a *sinner.* And who is there with wisdom sufficient to plumb this mystery? Christ was made this ugly thing we call "sin." All the sin ever committed and all the sin not yet committed was made to light on Him. God made His Son an offering for sin. And as He died as the Sin-Bearer, the Father in His holiness, had to turn His face away not from His Son, but from the terrible load of sin His holy One was bearing. Well might we pray:

> O help me understand, Lord
> What it meant for Thee
> To take my sin away.

APRIL 6

Who is holy, harmless, undefiled, separate from sinners...
higher than the heavens; who needeth not daily...to offer up
sacrifice, first for his own sins.
—Hebrews 7:26–27

Here we have multiplied evidence of our Lord's sinlessness. At least six descriptions are given of His unflecked holiness. He was holy—in His own inherent nature; harmless—in His dealings with men; undefiled—in His thoughts and feelings; separate from sinners—in His association with them in their manners and ways; higher than the heavens—in that the heavens are polluted by Satan's presence; no need to offer up a sacrifice for His own sins—seeing that He was without sin.

APRIL 7

The prince of this world cometh, and hath nothing in me.
—John 14:30

When Satan approaches us he has something to which he can appeal. A part of his territory is still within the possession of the old, natural life God has condemned. Satanic temptation, however, is unavailing as we claim victory on the ground of the cross, and allow the Holy Spirit to make over to us the holiness of our Lord. Satan had no ground within Christ he could call his own, seeing our Lord was holy in birth and practice. With you and me, Satan depends upon the fifth column of the flesh to aid him in the war against the Spirit-possessed life.

APRIL 8

Tempted…yet without sin.
—Hebrews 4:15

The question might be asked, "What was the purpose of our Lord's temptation if He was sinless and carried no possibility of sinning?" The answer is—Christ presented Himself to hell as well as earth as the sinless One, and such was too great a claim for the devil to leave unchallenged. So Christ suffered Himself to be tempted in all points, meaning along the three avenues of all temptation, namely, the lust of the flesh, the lust of the eye, and the pride of life. Temptation, by itself, is not sin. The children's hymn has it,

Yield not to temptation
For *yielding is* sin.
(lyric from "Yield Not to Temptation")

FIFTEENTH WEEK

OUR LORD'S DEATH

APRIL 9

They pierced my hands and my feet.
—Psalm 22:16

That Psalm 22 is called "the Calvary psalm" is proven by the fact that Jesus quoted it as He died in agony and shame. One of the remarkable features of this Psalm, written by David centuries before Christ was born, is the unique description it gives us of His inner anguish and outer suffering. No crucifixion narratives in the gospels give us such an intimate glimpse of all Calvary meant to Jesus. Here, in the phrase before us, we are told that His bountiful hands and beautiful feet were nail-pierced. What a strange reward for the work and walk of our holy Lord!

APRIL 10

It is expedient for us, that one man should die for the people,
and that the whole nation perish not.
—John 11:50

A study of John 11:47–52 makes it clear that Caiaphas, although among those who rejected Christ, yet under the Spirit's inspiration, predicted that Christ would die for the salvation of both Jews and Gentiles, and that the cross would destroy the partition-wall between them, bringing both together into one fold. The authoritative announcement of Caiaphas likewise contradicts the theory of a selective redemption. It also proves the substitutionary aspect of Calvary. Christ died for the people, so that they perish not.

APRIL 11

The Son of God, who loved me, and gave himself for me.
—Galatians 2:20

Nothing can fill the soul with gratitude like the endeavor to separate oneself from a world of teeming millions, and realize that while Christ died for all, He yet died for you and me, personally. Paul never got away from the personal aspect of the cross. That Christ loved him and died for him overpowered the apostle, and became the greatest incentive of his utter devotion to Jesus Christ. Loved me—gave Himself for *me*. Is it not the wonder of wonders that Christ should die for *you*? What was there in you to love? What virtue did Christ see in *you*, constraining Him to die for *you*? No merit of yours, only your misery drew forth the sacrifice of Calvary.

APRIL 12

Behold the Lamb of God, which taketh away the sin of the world.
—John 1:29

As he climbed Mount Moriah unconscious of the fact that he was to be offered as a sacrifice by his father, Isaac asked of Abraham, "*Where is the lamb?*" (Genesis 22:7). And in spite of the offering up of multitudinous lambs on Jewish altars, Isaac's question remains unanswered. It awaited a New Testament revelation. The question written all over the Old Testament is "*Where is the lamb?*" The central truth of the New Testament is "*Behold the Lamb of God!*" (John 1:35). The figure of the lamb takes us back to the Passover, when the lamb was slain, its life-blood sprinkled over the door post, and the family within saved and safe. Are you washed in the blood of the Lamb?

APRIL 13

Worthy is the Lamb that was slain.
—Revelation 5:12

The Pharisees thought that by killing Christ, His power would be terminated. Their confession was that "the world had gone after Him, and they could prevail nothing." And so the only way to destroy His popularity was to crucify Him. Little did they know that His cross would lead to His crown, that slaughter would bring Him sovereignty. The predominate truth of the Revelation is that a nail-pierced hand is to wield the scepter of universal dominion. The slain Lamb is the sovereign Lord. The Crucified is the Glorified. A thorn-scarred brow is diademed with many crowns. Such is the message of Easter.

APRIL 14

Baptized into his death.
—Romans 6:3

Holy Week, with all its remembrance of the cross and the empty tomb, will avail nothing unless it brings us into a fuller understanding and deeper experience of our union with Christ in His death and resurrection. What do we know about the fellowship of His sufferings and conformity to His death? Does this Easter season find us completely identified with our Lord in His death? When He died, I died. But am I dead—dead to the world, the flesh? Paul uses the word, *"buried"* (verse 4) in the passage before us. Buried! It is a grim term. If a person is dead and buried, they are out of sight, altogether so. Is this true of us, spiritually?

APRIL 15

God forbid that I should glory, save in the cross.
—Galatians 6:14

The apostle Paul turns from those who glory in the flesh to the only perfect object of boasting, namely, the old rugged cross. Glorying in the flesh and glorying in the cross do not mix. We cannot make much of the Crucified and of ourselves at the same time. The one glorying blasts the other. Paul could glory in the cross, seeing that it represented four sublime truths: A Law that had been satisfied, a love that had been manifested, a liberty that had been secured, and a Life that must be lived. Let us not lose sight of the three crosses Paul speaks of the cross on which Jesus died, the cross on which the world hangs, and the cross on which the saint is found.

SIXTEENTH WEEK

OUR LORD'S TRIUMPH

APRIL 16

It was not possible that he should be holden of it [death].
—Acts 2:24

While the Lord Jesus endured the pain of death and had death *upon* Him, the seed of death was not *in* Him. Being born in sin, we carry the seed of death. Sin, when it is finished, brings forth death. Jesus, however, was without sin and therefore without the death-principle within. As the Lord of life, then, He could not be holden of death.

APRIL 17

For this purpose the Son of God was manifested,
that he might destroy the works of the devil.
—1 John 3:8

In this selfsame chapter John reminds us that Christ was manifested to take away our sins. And triumph was His over sin and Satan! A perfect deliverance is ours in Him. Would that every pulpit in the land might publish abroad the taking away of sins and the destruction of the works of Satan!

Jesus is stronger than Satan and sin,
Satan to Jesus must bow;
Therefore I triumph without and within,

For Jesus saves me now.
(lyrics, "Jesus Hath Died and Hath Risen Again")

APRIL 18

And having spoiled principalities and powers, he made a shew
of them openly, triumphing over them in it.
—Colossians 2:15

The foes of our Lord gloated over the fact that they had succeeded in dragging Him to the cross. They spoiled Him, made a show of Him openly, triumphed over Him. But what actually happened is the truth Paul here glories in, namely, that Jesus laid hold of the dark, cruel forces of darkness and trailing them up the blood-red hill of Calvary, stripped them of their vaunted authority just as easily as young David tore the jaws of the lion. And that our sphere of conflict is in the same realm is evident from Ephesians 6:12.

APRIL 19

All power is given unto me in heaven and in earth.
—Matthew 28:18

Given unto Me! Who was it that delegated such absolute power to the risen Lord? It was the Father. Yet Jesus earned this power by His victorious death and resurrection. And is it not comforting to know that our Christ is supreme above and below? Why trouble ourselves about what we want from earth or heaven, when our Lord has sway over both realms?

Why should I charge my soul with care?
The wealth in every mine
Belongs to Christ, God's Son and Heir,
And He's a Friend of mine!
(lyric from "He's a Friend of Mine")

APRIL 20

He hath triumphed gloriously.
—Exodus 15:1, 21

The triumphs of would-be world rulers are usually inglorious. Bloodshed, tears, chaos, and destruction characterize their conquests. A trail of sorrow ever follows in their wake. But the triumphs of Christ are ever glorious. He never leaves anguish and heartaches behind. Righteously fought, His battles are ever beneficial in their outcome. As the result of His final conflict, sin, death, hell, and Satan will be deposited in the lake of fire forever and ever. And what a glorious triumph that will be!

APRIL 21

Thanks be unto God,
which always causeth us to triumph in Christ.
—2 Corinthians 2:14

One of the privileges we sometimes lose sight of as saints, is the fact that all Christ's triumphs are ours. All mine is thine. *"In Christ"* is a favorite expression in the Pauline epistles. It implies that all blessings from God are through Christ. And if we would triumph in life it can only be *"in Christ."* Can we say that His triumph is ours? Do we have the appropriating faith, making actual in life all that our glorious Victor made possible by His Calvary triumph?

APRIL 22

He led captivity captive, and gave gifts.
—Ephesians 4:8

By His ascension, our Lord made possible the glorious emancipation of the righteous, who, as prisoners of hope, had indwelt paradise or

Abraham's bosom from the time of their death. Before our Lord's death and resurrection, the place of departed spirits contained two sections—the abode of the righteous, known as above, and hell, the abode of the lost. The first compartment was emptied at the ascension, when Christ took all the righteous to heaven with Him. Hell remains the same, and will not be emptied and destroyed until the setting up of the great white throne. And thus, by His ascension, Christ earned the right to give gifts unto His own. Are you exercising your ascension gift?

SEVENTEENTH WEEK

THE SCRIPTURES

APRIL 23

All scripture is given by inspiration of God.
—2 Timothy 3:16

We believe that *all* means *all* and not some parts of the Bible. Modernism tells us that the Bible may *contain* the Word of God, but is not the Word of God in all its parts. And so we have shorter, mutilated Bibles. But Paul affirms that every part of the Scriptures is God-breathed.

Doubt regarding divine inspiration closes the door of revelation. The Bible is God's sensitive plant. The world's most effective preachers, teachers, and missionaries are those who hold the Scriptures to be divinely inspired from beginning to end.

APRIL 24

Thou hast known the holy scriptures.
—2 Timothy 3:15

Young Timothy was commended by the aged apostle for having a mind saturated with the Scriptures. From his earliest years, a godly mother had instructed Paul's son in the faith in the truths of the Word. And the value of such a privilege and advantage cannot be overestimated.

It is a sad reflection upon our modern home life when children are more anxious to read the "funnies" or "comic strips" than the Bible. As a parent are you creating a fascination for the incomparable stories of the incomparable Book in the mind of your child? If you familiarize children with the precious sayings of Jesus, the Holy Spirit has something to work on in after years.

APRIL 25

The law of the LORD *is perfect.*
—Psalm 19:7

Like their divine Author, the Scriptures are perfect or complete in every way. And, of course, by the Scriptures we mean the original manuscripts and not the translations. Extolling the perfection of the Word, David gives us a striking proof of its divine veracity and authority. It is able to convert the soul. If it were not perfect, it would be useless as a medium of salvation. Thus, every soul regenerated by the Spirit is a fresh evidence of the reliability of Scripture. A preacher who spends his gifts and time trying to undermine faith in the Bible's perfection is trying to fight with a broken sword.

APRIL 26

Thy word have I hid in mine heart.
—Psalm 119:11

Here we have the most precious provision *"Thy word"* in the most precious place *"mine heart"* for the most precious purpose *"not sin against thee."* Wealthy people, in order to guard their treasures from loss or theft, place them in strong bank vaults. Are we storing the precious promises of God within the vault of the mind, not merely that we might have accumulated treasure, but that in the hour of need such wealth might be immediately available?

We must go in for more Scripture memorizing if we would become more sinless. Defeated Christians are usually those who neglect to read and retain the Scriptures.

APRIL 27

Rightly dividing the word of truth.
—2 Timothy 2:15

Many religious creeds and cults sprang into being through a wrong division of Scripture. Isolated passages were stolen from the context and made the foundation of a sect. It would seem that misinterpretation arises through ignorance of what is known as "dispensational teaching." Saint Augustine declared that if we study the dispensations, the Scriptures will harmonize.

In our Bible study we must not be isolationists, but treat any part in the light of the whole. The Scriptures are not a mere arsenal of separate texts, any of which we may use as a peg upon which to hang some theory. They present a progressive and perfect revelation.

APRIL 28

While Peter yet spake these words.
—Acts 10:44

What an insight into effective evangelism this is. No hand-raising, no altar call, no coaxing or card-signing, but as Peter preached, the Holy Spirit performed the miracle of regeneration for the Gentiles. My preacher friend, do you not covet the power so to witness that, while preaching the glorious gospel, souls are converted?

Some phases of present-day evangelism are not only a racket but a positive hindrance to the Holy Spirit, Who always rides triumphant in His own chariot of the Scriptures.

APRIL 29

The seed is the word of God.
—Luke 8:11

The parable of the sower makes it clear that the sower, as such, is only responsible for the scattering of the seed and not for the harvest. The anxiety of some evangelists to butt heads in the matter of supposed conversions proves that they deem themselves responsible for results. Over-zealous sowers are guilty of counting numbers—the Holy Spirit produces numbers that count.

And, further, as seed, the Bible has life within itself. It describes itself as "the living Word." Seeds, however, although they possess inherent life, have to be sown in good soil and be wrought upon by the forces of nature ere they can germinate. Thus is it with the Word of God.

EIGHTEENTH WEEK

PRAYER

APRIL 30

He that cometh to God must believe that he is.
—Hebrews 11:6

Here we have two general principles regarding prayer, namely our conception of, and then our contact with, God. Contact depends upon conception. It is only if we know His name, or nature, as the Word implies, that we are able to trust Him. Our conception of God must be twofold: We must believe He is real (that He is) and also a Rewarder of those who accept His reality.

Is God real to you? Do you believe that He rewards those who seek Him? The diligence of your search and the blessedness of your contact depend upon your understanding of God's grace, goodness, and greatness.

MAY 1

Lord, teach us to pray.
—Luke 11:1

While it is true that men, even godless men, cry to God in the deep crises of life, the fact remains that prayer is not natural to man. He has to be instructed in such a holy art, by the very One he desires to approach. And prayer depends upon relationship. It was as *disciples* that one of them prayed, *"Lord, teach us to pray."* To address a man as "father" implies sonship. Have you been born into the family of God? Can you call Jesus *Lord*? Effectual prayer is ever a result of making Jesus the Lord of our life.

MAY 2

Praying always with all prayer.
—Ephesians 6:18

Outside an English church the sign was found: "When your knees knock, kneel on them." But we should not only pray when we come to an emergency. Prayer is not merely a fire escape from danger, it is our vital breath. So as Paul reminds us, we are to pray always. Can we say that prayer is our native air?

It would seem as if the apostle duplicates his words here. *"Praying always with all prayer."* The qualifying clause is at the end: in the Spirit. We are never in the spirit of prayer unless the Spirit is in our prayer. There is a vast difference between saying prayers and praying. Which do you practice?

MAY 3

We know not what we should pray for.
—Romans 8:26

How helpless we are without our indwelling intercessor, the Holy Spirit! At the best we are only "Infants, crying in the night with no language but a cry" ("In Memoriam A.H.H." by Tennyson). Knowing the mind of God, the Spirit can enable us to present our petitions accordingly. He it is who takes our sighs, broken and imperfect utterances, and recasts them, until they rise as sweet incense before God.

And what we are prone to forget as we approach the mercy seat, where *Jesus* answers prayers, is that the Father ever responds to our prayers not according to our intelligence but according to His own. So often we ask but receive not, seeing we ask amiss.

MAY 4

Sin…in ceasing to pray.
—1 Samuel 12:23

We seldom catalog prayerlessness as a sin, grievous in the sight of the Lord. Samuel, however, knew that if he failed to pray for the idolatrous multitude he would be guilty of sinning against the Lord, and the people who needed his prayers. Salvation carries with it a solemn obligation. Being saved implies the responsibility of trying to save others. Do you realize that you are debtor to those around you, and that if you cease to pray and labor for their ingathering, then you sin against them?

Praying without ceasing for the lost is an arduous task. George Muller prayed for well-nigh fifty years for a soul.

MAY 5

Whatsoever ye shall ask in prayer, believing.
—Matthew 21:22

Christ here gives us a blank check: *"Whatsoever."* Surely this covers all our need. How slow we are to cash our check. But let it be noticed that prayer will only be answered as it accompanied by faith. Have you faith to praise God for the assurance of granted requests, even though the answers have not yet reached earth? Doubtless you have heard of the old lady who had a small hill in front of her windows that somewhat obscured her outlook. Taking our Lord's Word about prayer moving mountains a little too literally, she asked for the troublesome hill to be removed. Waking up next morning and finding the hill still there she remarked, "Just as I thought."

MAY 6

Labouring fervently for you in prayers.
—Colossians 4:12

Epaphras, oft commended by Paul, must have been one of the finest Christians in the early church. He was certainly a prayer warrior. He knew how to pray through. To him prayer was a ministry. Dr. C. I. Scofield has the note under the verse above, "A touching illustration of priestly service as distinguished from ministry of gift. Shut up in prison, no longer able to preach, Epaphras was still equally with all believers, a priest. No prison could keep him from the throne of grace, so he gave himself wholly to the priestly work to intercession."

NINETEENTH WEEK

FAITH

MAY 7

Faith is the substance of things hoped for.
—Hebrews 11:1

What we have here is not a definition of faith but a declaration of its action. Faith is certain the ship is coming to port although it cannot be seen. The eleventh chapter of Hebrews, called "the Westminster Abbey of the Bible," is a remarkable dissertation on "*faith.*" We have the path of faith in 11:1–7; the patience of faith, 11:8–22; the power of faith, 11:23–40; the pattern of faith, 12:1–2. Faithful means full of faith.

MAY 8

Have faith in God.
—Mark 11:22

Sometimes we hear it argued that it does not matter what a man believes, so long as he believes something. But what we believe in shapes our character and determines destiny, so it makes a great deal of difference what we fix our faith on. A gangster has his faith. He believes that he should live by plundering others of their possessions. His belief, however, makes him a menace to society.

Our Lord gives us the perfect object of faith, an object gracing life with His own beauty. Have faith in *God.* Have faith in—! What follows "*in*" either enriches or impoverishes life.

MAY 9

God hath dealt to every man the measure of faith.
—Romans 12:3

That faith is God's gift and that to some is granted more than to others is evident from the Bible and experience. All of us have faith, but some of us have a greater measure than others. And to whom much is given, much is expected.

Four times over our Lord spoke of *"little faith"* as a condition characteristic of His disciples. (See Matthew 6:30, 8:26, 14:31, 16:8.) Toplady said, "'Little Faith' goes to heaven no less than 'Great Faith,' though not so comfortably."

"According to your faith, be it unto you" (Matthew 9:29). Such a declaration suggests an expanding mercy: it implies the necessity of seeking an ever-enlarging measure of trust in the power of the faithfulness of God. As God gives faith, may we be led to go in for a full supply.

MAY 10

Strong in faith, giving glory to God…
—Romans 4:20

Dr. Weymouth's translation has it, "Under hopeless circumstances, he hopefully believed." He staggered not! Abraham believed that God could cause the impossible to happen. Do you? "Act faith," our forefathers used to say. The late General William Booth's slogan was "Keep up with your repeated act of faith." The old Methodist preacher gave us practical wisdom when he wrote, "If the devil puts up a stone wall in front us we are to believe right through it." Combining these sayings we come to the secret of strong faith. By repeated *acts* of faith we come to *act* faith, and believe, thereby, right through all stone walls.

MAY 11

The trial of your faith.
—1 Peter 1:7

Such a trial is exemplified in the lives of Abraham, Joseph, the prophets, and the apostle Paul. (See Genesis 22:1, 2; 40:14, 15; Psalm 105:17, 19; 2 Corinthians 11:24–28.) Jesus tried the nobleman Capernaum who was deeply concerned about his sick son. *"Except ye see signs and wonders, ye will not believe"* (John 4:48). The nobleman's faith in Christ's ability won the day, even though it was tested. Reaching home, he found faith translated into fact. Within the narrative we have personal faith (verse 50); progressive faith (verse 51); prevailing faith (verses 52 and 53). Is your faith being severely, sorely tried? Keep believing! God is ever near no matter how dark the night.

MAY 12

Whether ye be in the faith.
—2 Corinthians 13:5

We must distinguish between "faith" as a principle of and "faith" as a body of revealed truth. The former, of course is made possible by the latter. When we speak of one as losing the "faith" we mean that he rejects the revealed truth of God. There is *"one faith"* (Ephesians 4:5) and for such we are to *"earnestly contend"* (Jude 1:3).

No person can have faith, as we know it, unless he holds *"the faith which was once delivered unto the saints"* (Jude 1:3). The modernist, attacking and denying the fundamental facts of the faith, is not conspicuous for his faith and confidence in God. He is usual self-centered and self-satisfied.

MAY 13

The fruit of the Spirit...is faith.
—Galatians 5:22

Whether faith is the opening of a beggar's hand to receive the gold of heaven, or active energy in devotion, or the bridge across the chasm between the soul and God, it is ever the gift and fruit of the Holy Spirit. Of course, we have a natural faith which we exercise apart altogether from grace. When we deposit our letters in the mail box we believe they will reach their destination. Boarding a train, we believe it will carry us to where we are going. Faith, however, to believe that we are lost and need a Savior, and that Christ by His death and resurrection can save us, is a gift imparted by the Spirit.

TWENTIETH WEEK

HOLINESS

MAY 14

Be ye holy; for I am holy.
—1 Peter 1:16

Peter's heart-moving appeal for holiness is based upon the holy character of God. *"As he which hath called you is holy, so be ye holy"* (verse 15). And *"glorious in holiness,"* (Exodus 15:11), God is not only the foundation and pattern of holiness, but the Source of our holiness. What He commands, He supplies. And so, as Augustine put it, "Give what Thou commandest, and then command what Thou wilt." Here God commands us to be holy and He graciously supplies the very holiness, glorifying to His name.

MAY 15

Holiness becometh thine house, O LORD, forever.
—Psalm 93:5

While we may not have very much sympathy with the rites, ceremonies and liturgies in Roman and High church circles, we have to confess that they often have an atmosphere conducive to worship, such as we do not have in some of our Protestant churches. Certainly we do not go in for robes, vestments, incense, candles, and prayers. But surely we should cultivate reverence, such as is characteristic of churches extremely ritualistic. Why, we have to placard our church vestibules with notices about being silent! Roman Catholics are not so reminded. Protestants are guilty of laxity, thoughtlessness, and irreverence, when it comes to church behavior. The few minutes before a service begins suggest the rabble of a market rather than the sanctuary where a holy God waits to reveal Himself. Paul has a pointed word about behaving ourselves in the church of God. (See 1 Timothy 3:15.)

MAY 16

The spirit of holiness.
—Romans 1:4

It may be that one reason why the third person of the Trinity is called "the Holy Spirit" so often in the Bible is because His great task is to transform us into the holiness of God. "Every thought of holiness is His alone." As the *Holy* Spirit, He is deeply grieved when anything is entertained within our life alien to His holy mind and will. Do we please or pain the Spirit? In Ephesians 4:25–32 we are given a list of fleshly traits that grieve Him. Run your finger down the catalogue and see if you stand condemned.

MAY 17

Upon...the pots...holiness unto the LORD.
—Zechariah 14:20–21

What can the insignia of holiness upon bells and pots mean but that the Lord expects our commercial and social life to bear the imprint of our allegiance to Him? In a land like America where horses are so few in comparison with the millions of automobiles in use, we can change the figure and say, "Upon every car, holiness unto the Lord." Is yours a consecrated car? Do you use it in His service and for His glory, as well as for your own pleasure? And, holiness upon every pot implies that the home will always be clean and tidy. Sister, the next time you are tempted to grumble about so many pots and pans to wash up, remember that the kitchen can be turned into a sanctuary if the glory the Lord is brought into the most commonplace duties!

MAY 18

Difference between holy and unholy.
—Leviticus 10:10

Many of the Mosaic enactments were necessary to prove that the Jews were a separated people. By their religious observance camp life, food and raiment, they were conspicuously different from surrounding heathen nations. Our tragedy is that of conformity to the world. As professed Christians, we are not as distinctive as we should be. Separation from the pleasures and pursuits of an unholy world is not as marked as the Scriptures demand. Is your life different? Those around you make a claim of being saved. Do they wonder why you should make a profession of religion as they notice that their worldly desires, joys, and ambitions are yours? May we all experience with Mary Slessor, the famous missionary, that "complete separation from the world spells power for God!"

MAY 19

What manner of persons ought ye to be.
—2 Peter 3:11

The apostle Peter urges the coming of the Lord as a powerful incentive to personal holiness. And, truly, when we remember that Christ may be here at any moment, we find ourselves stirred to purity of life. John emphasizes a similar truth when he tells us that if we live under the power of the blessed hope, we will be pure even as Christ Himself is pure (See 1 John 3:1–3.) Holy conversation! Does our language reveal the residence of the King within? Is our speech attractive because of its divine accent? But as *"conversation"* is used here, it implies our manner of life, and may lips and life be influenced by the return of Christ.

MAY 20

By our...holiness we had made this man to walk.
—Acts 3:12

In the first apostolic miracle, Peter wanted it to be known that the lame man was directly healed by God. It was not by any personal virtues any of the apostles possessed that the beggar rose up and walked. The bystanders were not to marvel over the miracle as if by his own power of holiness Peter had made it possible. Nevertheless, Peter's life contributed to the miracle. The channel must correspond to the source. God's holy work is accomplished by holy workmen. *"The life was the light of men"* (John 1:4). Life and light! Yes, the Life never fails to illuminate the minds of men. It is not so much what we say but the Life pulsating through the message that counts for God.

TWENTY-FIRST WEEK

OUR OWN HOUSEHOLD

MAY 21

A man's foes…his own household.
—Matthew 10:36

A characteristic feature of our Lord's teaching is the fact that it passed through the crucible of experience. And truth is ever effective when it is wrung out of one's own heart. Variance in home life over allegiance to God on the part of some members within the home was what Jesus endured for almost twenty years as He lived in His humble Nazareth home. At the early age of twelve, He had to rebuke His mother for failure to understand His divine mission. Others around Him did not believe in Him. He was an alien to His brethren and as a stranger to His mother's children.

MAY 22

The earth opened her mouth, and swallowed…their households.
—Deuteronomy 11:6

Surely nothing is comparable to the tragedy of a home in which all are partners in sin. Godless homes are dread foes of good communal life. Godly homes make for prosperity in every realm. Homes without grace or God may appear to be happy and prosperous, but certain judgment awaits them. Hell will be enlarged to receive them. As Mahan and Abiram, the sons of Eliab, are specifically named, it would seem as if they had fashioned their respective worthless homes. As a father, what kind of a home are you creating?

MAY 23

Without honour, but…in his own house.
—Mark 6:4

The rejection of Christ's claims by His own kith and kin was His deepest stab. Truly, He came as a prophet, yet no honor reached Him from the family of which He formed part. Multiplied honors came to Him from others, but among His brothers and sisters He was unrecognized. Is this your cross? Because of the lack of spiritual understanding, those nearest you do not appreciate your allegiance to Jesus Christ, nor your passion to witness for Him. Your closest friends slight you, and treat you somewhat indifferently. Outside of your home there are like-minded souls who value your witness and who honor you for all you mean to them in spiritual things. Well, such is the price of discipleship.

MAY 24

But he [Lot] seemed as one that mocked.
—Genesis 19:14

Lot paid a dear price for pitching his tent toward Sodom. Once within such a godless city he married a worldly-minded woman and succumbed to the carnal atmosphere surrounding him. The incestuousness of his two daughters reveals the low moral tone of home and city. Roused at last to the certainty of divine judgment, upon the Sodomites, Lot sought to warn his own, only to be treated with contempt. As a Christian, have you formed alliances that have silenced your testimony? Beware! The day will come when your own flesh and blood will mock your warning. Whatever it costs, get right with God now, and whether your loved ones repent or not, so live as to be a constant rebuke to their godlessness.

MAY 25

His [Samuels's] *sons walked not in his ways.*
—1 Samuel 8:3

Paternal pride, even in a godly man like Samuel, led him in his old age to commit the fatal blunder of placing his godless sons in a position demanding uprightness and integrity. And godless sons of a godly father ever exert a pernicious influence. It was because of the perversion of justice on the part of Samuel's sons that the elders of Israel turned from a theocracy to a monarchy. No matter how good a preacher a man may be, somehow his ministry is hindered in its effectiveness if he is the father of unconverted children. Are these lines being read by those who, like Joel and Abijah, know not the Lord? Well, why not chase the wrinkles from off the brow of a saintly parent with the good news, "*Thy God* [shall be] *my God*" (Ruth 1:16)?

MAY 26

Notwithstanding, they hearkened not unto the voice of their father.
—1 Samuel 2:25

The sons of Eli the priest are described as "base," and "*abhorred* [despised] *the offering of the* LORD," (verse 17) "*lay with the women that* [did service] *assembled at the door of the* [tent of meeting] *tabernacle*" (verse 25). Thus they were irreligious and iniquitous. And, truly, their evil practices were enough to break a father's heart. But Eli's reproofs were unavailing. Severe judgment overtook his godless offspring. Among the mysterious things of life is the fact that there are many praying parents who weep over children lost in sin, in spite of groans and tears cannot see any sign of repentance in those they love. Hell will be all the more terrible if a father's prayers and entreaties rise up to haunt one.

MAY 27

Esau...a grief of mind unto Isaac and to Rebekah.
—Genesis 26:34, 35

By taking two wives from the Hittites, Esau sinned against divine light, and at the same time deeply grieved his god-fearing mother and father. Their holy wishes were crossed. Have you wayward children who are opposite to you in all things? Pleadings on your part, not to countenance those pleasures and pursuits contrary to your Christian principles, are unavailing. Pray on, disappointed one! God has a father's heart, and sooner than you expect He may cause your family circle to be complete in grace.

TWENTY-SECOND WEEK

THE WORLD

MAY 28

In the world ye shall have tribulation...I have overcome the world.
—John 16:33

Jesus never offered His own an easy path. All the words associated with discipleship are "blood" words: Taking up crosses, reproach, false accusations, hazarding the life, persecution, and tribulation. Living in a world satanically controlled, the believer must be prepared to endure some of its misery. Being a Christian does not guarantee immunity from the trials and sorrows of the world. He has, however, a hiding place of which the worldling is ignorant: *"In me,"* tribulation in the world, tranquility in Him.

MAY 29

The victory that overcometh the world...our faith.
—1 John 5:4

John makes it clear that there are three characteristic features of world conquerors: born of God, faith, and belief that Jesus is the Son of God. And, truly, such a threefold cord makes us invincible. The threefold repetition of *"overcometh the world"* indicates its importance. Would we be found among the valiant overcomers, treading under foot all worldly practices and pursuits, then we must be born again, strong in our faith in God's ability, firm in our grasp of the deity of Christ.

MAY 30

What is a man profited, if he shall gain the whole world,
and lose his own soul?
—Matthew 16:26

Many years ago I came across the lines…

The clock of life is wound but once
And no man has the power
To tell just when the clock will stop
At late or early hour.

To lose one's wealth is sad indeed,
To lose one's health is more,
To lose one's soul is such a loss
That no man can restore.
("The Clock of Life" by Robert H. Smith)

Only one life
'Twill soon be past
Only what's done for Christ will last.
("Only One Life", by C. T. Studd)

The more of the world we gain, the more of our soul we lose. What are material and physical gains worth if they result in spiritual loss! All the world can offer is only for a time, and ends with the grave. Our souls are destined for eternity. And who, with any wisdom, would barter temporal, worldly benefits for eternal treasures?

MAY 31

The god of this world.
—2 Corinthians 4:4

The warrior's foes are infernal, as well as internal, external, and fraternal. Arrayed against him are *"the rulers of the darkness of this world"*

(Ephesians 6:12); *"the prince of this world"* (John 14:30; 16:11); and *"the kingdoms of the world"* (Matthew 4:8). And that blindness to spiritual realities, on the part of the multitudes, is of Satan whom Paul calls *"the god of this world,"* (2 Corinthians 4:4) is evident on every hand. And that Satan uses things, both good and bad, in the world to keep the soul in darkness is fully understood by those who have spiritual discernment. But although "the god of this world," he is yet subject to the God who overcame the world.

JUNE 1

Demas hath forsaken me, having loved this present world.
—2 Timothy 4:10

Have you ever noticed the two loves Paul places together? In verse eight he speaks of those who love Christ's appearing and in verse ten of those who love this world. Love His appearing! Love this present world! What a study in contrasts! We cannot entertain these two loves at the same time. The one must yield to the other. Loving His appearing blasts the love of the world. On the other hand, love for the world destroys our love for Christ's return. Which love dominates your heart? Can it be that you have degenerated into a Demas? (See Romans 12:2; James 1:27.)

JUNE 2

Godly, in this present world.
—Titus 2:12

Sometimes we are challenged by the statement that it is impossible to be a true Christian in a world like ours. Well, Paul taught otherwise. Ungodliness and worldly lusts can be scorned and grace is ours to live victoriously, whether it be inward (soberly) outward (righteously) or godward (godly) in this present world. And that such a victory can be ours is based upon the cross, seeing that Christ *"gave himself for our sins that he might deliver us from this present evil world"* (Galatians 1:4).

JUNE 3

As he is, so are we in this world.
—1 John 4:17

John had clear ideas as to the believer's association with the world. And in an age when separation is not a palatable message, John's explicit declarations are unwanted. Recording Christ's prayer he reminds us that we *"are not of the world, even as I [Christ] am not of the world"* (John 17:16). And again, *"if any man love the world, the love of the Father is not in him"* (1 John 2:15). A certain test as to whether we should engage in worldly pleasures is to ask ourselves the question, "What would Jesus do if He were in my place?"

TWENTY-THIRD WEEK

THE FLESH

JUNE 4

The garment spotted by the flesh.
—Jude 23

Carnal and *fleshly* are Paul's words for the Adamic nature and for the believer who "walks," that is, lives under the power of it—flesh, in the ethical sense, is the whole natural or unregenerate man, spirit, soul, and body, as centered upon self, prone to sin, and opposed to God. The regenerate man is not in (the sphere of) the flesh but in (the sphere of) the Spirit, but the flesh is still in him, and he may, according to his choice, "*walk after the flesh*" or "*after the Spirit*" (Romans 8:1). In the first case, he is a "carnal" and in the second a "spiritual" Christian. Victory over the flesh will be the habitual experience of the believer who walks in the Spirit.

JUNE 5

That which is born of the flesh is flesh.
—John 3:6

We would look upon a farmer who sowed potatoes and expected a harvest of apples as being a fit subject for a lunatic asylum. Potatoes can only produce potatoes; and the flesh, nothing but the flesh. Regeneration is not the improvement of the old nature, but the impartation of a new nature altogether. Salvation by character is an effort to get apples out of potatoes. The flesh, even when cultured and religious, can never produce what the Holy Spirit alone can bring to pass. This was the hard truth Nicodemus had to learn. (See also Galatians 6:8; 2 Corinthians 10:3.)

JUNE 6

If ye live after the flesh, ye shall die.
—Romans 8:13

In the realm of the Spirit the deeds of the flesh are brought to the place of death. The story is told of an aviator who, while navigating his machine, heard a rattle that troubled him. Looking around, he discovered a rat gnawing away at a vital part of the airplane. Evidently while it was grounded, the machine offered a safe harbor for the rat and it remained unnoticed while the aviator was leaving the ground, and until he was well on his journey. What was he to do? He could not stop to kill the rat. Upward he shot, knowing that in the rarer air the rat could not live. And sure enough, it fell over dead. Have you discovered that in the higher, purer air of the Spirit fleshly desires cannot live?

JUNE 7

As many as desire to make a fair shew in the flesh…
—Galatians 6:12

Paul gave no quarter to those who gloried *"after the flesh"* (2 Corinthians 11:18). If any had a reasonable right to glory in a Jewish heritage, it *was* the apostle, but in Christ he died to such, and gloried only in the cross. Marks on the flesh are a poor substitution for the inner circumcision of the heart is the teaching of Paul in his Galatian epistle. A good deal of the ritual practiced in certain religious circles is of the flesh, and caters to the flesh. Those who are willing to endure persecution for the cross of Christ are not deeply concerned about forms, vestments incense, candles, and meaningless prayers.

JUNE 8

They that are in the flesh cannot please God.
—Romans 8:8

It should be the undying passion of every believer to please God. Jesus could confess, "*I do always those things that please him* [my Father]" (John 8:29) because He never satisfied carnal desires. In verse nine Paul has two phrases that afford a contrast, namely, "*In the flesh...in the Spirit*" (verse 9). If in the flesh, we are not in the Spirit, and vice versa. Our blessed Lord ever lived in the Spirit and was never, therefore, in the flesh. Let us not grieve the heart of God by the countenance of those ways of the flesh resulting in the death of spiritual desires.

JUNE 9

The works of the flesh are manifest.
—Galatians 5:19

What an evil offspring the flesh produces! But over against "*the works of the flesh*" Paul places "*the fruit of the Spirit*" (verses 22–23). And if Christ's, the flesh with its affections and lusts are on a cross. What does your life manifest—works or fruit? Paul's emphasis of the Holy Spirit's ministry in our deliverance should be noted. It is He Who, through the new nature, keeps the old nature in the place of daily death. The works of the flesh are ever dormant within the believer, but he constantly dies to them by the grace of the Spirit, Who in turn produces true Christian graces.

JUNE 10

Fire out of the rock...consumed the flesh.
—Judges 6:21

In what the angel of God accomplished for Gideon we have a fitting type of the basis of our victory over all the ways and works of the carnal nature. Fire is one of the symbols of the Holy Spirit. The smitten rock is a type of Christ. Fire came out of the Rock, meaning that Pentecost came as the result of Calvary. Had there been no smitten Rock, there could have been no Fire. But now the Fire out of the Rock can consume the flesh. Self-effort or self-suppression can never produce victory. Apart from the blood of the Rock and the Fire of the Spirit, we are both helpless and hopeless in the conflict. The emblem of salvation is "Blood and Fire." And every saint needs both.

TWENTY-FOURTH WEEK

THE DEVIL

JUNE 11

Being forty days tempted of the devil.
—Luke 4:2

The word *"devil"* comes from a word meaning "to throw down." And, true to his name, Satan ever strives to cast us down. He wanted Jesus to cast Himself down from the pinnacle of the temple. The devil is a destroyer of character, life, and nations. The Lord, however, is spoken of as the *"lifter up"* (Psalm 3:3) of our head. Heaven elevates—hell exterminates.

JUNE 12

And he laid hold on the dragon, that old serpent,
which is the Devil.
—Revelation 20:2

The designations of the devil reveal his diabolical character. As the *"dragon"* he is fierce and cruel. As the *"serpent"* he is subtle and crafty. And let us never forget that he has the accumulated wisdom of well-nigh six millenniums. Profiting by his mistakes, he has had ample time to perfect his crafty designs against God and man. In ourselves we are no match for his hellish wisdom. But *"greater is he that is in you than he that is in the world"* (1 John 4:4).

JUNE 13

The Devil…was cast out into the earth.
—Revelation 12:9

The biography of Satan can be told in a few words. Originally a highly exalted angelic being, he coveted God's throne. As the leader of a revolt in heaven he was deposed and has since had the air as his abode. John reminds us that he is to be forced from the air to the earth, and woe to the inhabitants of the earth when this takes place. At the setting up of the millennium he is to be cast into the bottomless pit. After the thousand years he is to be released yet a little season, and then comes his eternal abode in the lake of fire. Satan is therefore a prodigal son of God's for whom there is no return.

JUNE 14

Resist the devil, and he will flee from you.
—James 4:7

The secret of resistance is clearly defined by James. It is submission to God. We must read the text as a whole. Submission to God means that we leave Him to deal with the devil. He has little fear of us. He does, however, fear the mighty God within us. And panoplied thus with the power of heaven we have the prerogative to say, *"Get thee behind me, Satan"* (Matthew 16:23). Divinely-inspired resistance means retreat for the devil. He only leaves us, however, for a season. Defeated, he returns with greater fury to overcome us. But clad in the whole armor of God, we are able to withstand all satanic assaults.

JUNE 15

Satan cometh immediately, and taketh away the word.
—Mark 4:15

Cognizant of human weakness to depend upon the arm of the flesh, the devil has succeeded from Adam's day to induce man to rely upon his own strength and possessions. For his reliance upon thousands of valiant men, David displeased God and merited His judgment. Some evangelists and pastors are prone to depend far too much upon numbers. Quite recently a church was encountered whose preacher has a small adding machine by which an usher can check the numbers attending the church. Well, it is better to have numbers that count than merely to count numbers!

JUNE 16

Satan cometh immediately, and taketh away the word.
—Mark 4:15

The devil goes to church, and when he does, it is to prey and not to pray. Alas, we do not realize that he is present every time the Word is preached in order to destroy the work of the Trinity in salvation and sanctification. Of course, Satan never hurries to churches given over to modernism. There is nothing in such to trouble his kingdom. But wherever the truth is preached in the power of the Holy Spirit sent down from heaven, then dark and destructive, hellish forces are active. If you are a preacher, is your preaching a constant source of annoyance to Satan?

JUNE 17

Satan hath desired to have you, that he may sift you as wheat.
—Luke 22:31

The Savior and Satan are the rival bidders for the complete control of the saint. I am my Beloved's and His *desire* is toward me—"*Satan hath desired to have you.*" Christ desires our holiness. Satan desires our defeat and misery. In his sifting, Peter lost the chaff of self-confidence. Is Satan sifting you? Well, live near to the heart of God so that the precious wheat of faith will abide the test. Satan, an old writer has reminded us, leads us down a winding staircase. One step follows the other and we never know when the final end is. Then, let us watch the first step!

TWENTY-FIFTH WEEK

THE MAN FACE

JUNE 18

...the face of a man.
—Ezekiel 1:10

In his symbolism of the living creatures, Ezekiel commences with the likeness of a man, which is as it should be, seeing man is the head of all things material. Dominion has been granted him. (See Psalm 8:6.)

This particular face signifies conscience, intellect, sympathy, love, and all the best in humanity. And the world is quick in responding to the magnetism of a sanctified humaneness. Do you feel that you are not as manly as you ought to be? Are you unsympathetic, selfish, or mean? Is the cry of your heart, "O that a man may arise in me, so that the man I am may cease to be?" ("Maud," by Alfred Tennyson). Well, just put on the new man more completely, and then wear the face of a true man.

JUNE 19

Come, see a man.
—John 4:29

That true manhood was Christ's is evidenced by the fact that the woman of Sychar felt she had met One who was out to enrich her character and not damage it. Men had abused her, but *the Man*, who told her all things about her guilty past, sought her highest welfare.

And truly, Jesus was a Man approved of God. Found in fashion as a Man, He ever remained the best of men. Sympathy of heart and strength of character must have been written upon His countenance. He was no "sissy," to use a modern vulgarism. Impressed with His courage, a brave soldier like the centurion confessed, *"Truly this man was the Son of God"* (Mark 15:39).

JUNE 20

Is a man better than a sheep?
—Matthew 12:12

While many men are about as silly and senseless as sheep, the fact remains that a man is better than a sheep for at least three reasons. First, man was made in the image of God and therefore has faculties that sheep never had. Then, man is immortal, while the death of a sheep is its end. In the third place, Christ died for men, and not for sheep. The tragedy, however, is the truth Isaiah declares, namely, that a man in his sin is no better than a sheep nibbling away at the grass around, unconscious of any danger ahead.

JUNE 21

The Lord is a man of war.
—Exodus 15:3

From a womanly man and a manly woman may the good Lord deliver us! Determination to tread down all evil forces is certainly a manly virtue. Some men are too effeminate to raise their voices in protest against those vices their conscience condemns. But no such weakness is the Lord's. *"The Lord shall go forth as a mighty man, he shall stir up jealousy like a man of war: he shall cry, yea, roar; he shall prevail against his enemies"* (Isaiah 42:13).

As a man, are you making war against sin and Satan? Dr. Hugh Price Hughes, the renowned English Methodist minister, once urged a young pastor to make himself a nuisance until every nuisance was put down. Our encouragement to strike out against all that is ruinous to a man is the counsel of Joshua.

JUNE 22

A man shall be as an hiding place.
—Isaiah 32:2

Surely there is no other who answers to the prophet's description of beneficial manhood like the Man who, because He continues forever, hath an unchangeable priesthood. It is He Who is able to help distressed humanity to the uttermost.

Becoming a Man, the Lord Jesus understands the needs of men and offers Himself accordingly as the unfailing source of consolation and succor. And what impressive metaphors are used to describe the intimate care Jesus affords: hiding place, covert, rivers of water, the shadow of a great rock. My fellow believer, remember, whatever your human needs may be, that Jesus has a human heart that feels and cares!

JUNE 23

A man sent from God, whose name was John.
—John 1:6

When God finds the man He desires to use, He never rests until He fashions and fills that man. Whom He elects, He graciously equips. And because He condescends to take up men like ourselves, may we not fail Him in this hour of great need. He alone is able to save souls, but He saves them through those He sends. Are you a sent one? Commissioned by God, are you functioning as a true ambassador?

D. L. Moody was a man sent by God. And the crisis for world-wide service came when he heard a friend remark, "The world has yet to see what God can do through a man utterly yielded to His will."

JUNE 24

The Son of man hath not where to lay his head.
—Matthew 8:20

Here is our Lord's general designation while He is called "The Son of God"—"The Son of His love"—"The Son." He is named *"The Son of man"* over eighty times by the evangelists. This is our Lord's racial name as the representative Man, and is the term He uses when speaking of His mission, death, resurrection and Second Advent. It is in this name also, that universal judgment is committed unto Him. It is also a name indicating that in Him is fulfilled the Old Testament fore view of blessing through a coming Man. (For full references see Scofield's comment.)

TWENTY-SIXTH WEEK

THE OX FACE

JUNE 25

...the face of an ox...
—Ezekiel 1:10

The ox represents the head of tame beasts. It is lord of the field and the king of pasture. Patience, meekness, gentleness, and yet strength are symbolized by the ox. An ancient motto has the figure of an ox with a plough on one side and an altar on the other, and the inscription, "Ready for either." Service or sacrifice make no difference to the ox. (See Proverbs 7:22; 14:4.)

Is the patience of the ox ours? Because "the mills of God grind slowly" ("Retribution," by Wadsworth Longfellow), we have need of patience with heaven. God is never in a hurry. And then, we need to be patient toward all men. Alas, we are guilty of hurried conclusions and hasty criticisms. Coming to ourselves, we need to possess our souls in patience. When we feel like putting the hands of the clock forward, let ours be the face and nature of the ox.

JUNE 26

Thou shalt not plow with an ox and an ass together.
—Deuteronomy 22:10

The law of separation is herewith symbolized and enforced. As the nature and steps of the creatures named are totally different, to place an ass and an ox together would greatly hinder the service of the latter. And what is this but the truth of separation as taught by Paul where he warns us about being unequally yoked together with unbelievers? For a believer to be in fellowship with an unbeliever in any capacity whatever is for the ox and ass to plow together. How can two walk and witness together except they be agreed?

JUNE 27

Thou shalt not muzzle the ox when he treadeth out the corn.
—Deuteronomy 25: 4

If the ox is to render its best service it must be untrammeled. Unnecessary harness and trappings would hinder progress. The beast must be free of encumbrances if its master desires the best labor.

Are you free to serve? Some there are who find themselves overloaded with details. Trivialities dominate their time and attention. Called to tread out corn, their energy is spent on trill. Many a minister is muzzled by denominationalism. And nothing is so tragic as the plight of a man who in his heart knows the truth but who, for the sake of peace and position, he is muzzled. Are you fettered or free? (See 1 Corinthians 9:7–9.)

JUNE 28

The ox knoweth his master.
—Isaiah 1:3

It is surprising how dumb creatures respond to human kindness. A beast can discern his master's voice and walk, and respond immediately to his command. Watch a farmer with his animals! Although under his feet, he yet treats them not as equals but as creatures capable of response.

God's complaint against His own was that they did not come nor consider Him. An ox will turn its head and welcome the affectionate treatment of its master, but human beings, more highly endowed than oxen, and the recipients of divine care and provision, can be capable of heartless rejection. God's continual sorrow is that children He nourishes and brings up rebel against Him. Do you know and love your Master?

JUNE 29

What meaneth…the lowing of the oxen which I hear.
—1 Samuel 15:14

Because of their harsh dealings with Israel, Saul was commanded to slay all that the Amalekites had, but as one brought up among cattle, his feelings for the best of the oxen got the better of him. Kindness led to compromise. Saul's sin, however, was more than incomplete obedience. The lowing of the ox reaching Samuel's ears proved that he had lied. God told him to utterly destroy all, and spare not. Meeting Samuel, Saul says *"I have obeyed the voice of the LORD"* (verse 20). But the bleating sheep and lowing oxen told another story. Let us beware of an incomplete and false consecration.

JUNE 30

The consecrated things were six hundred oxen.
—2 Chronicles 29:33

Although beasts of burden, the oxen employed in temple worship were among its hallowed things. Their association with the altar as burnt offerings consecrated them. All of which teaches us that if we are the Lord's, then all about us should bear the imprint of consecration. Possessions, as well as persons, can be set aside for God. We may be in humble circumstances, doing humble things, yet if we are truly saved, even insignificant lives and tasks can glorify God.

JULY 1

Which of you shall have...an ox fallen into a pit,
and will not straightway pull him out?
—Luke 14:5

If God cares for the oxen (see 1 Corinthians 9:9), we ought to deal kindly with them, both for His sake and their own. The meanest of God's creatures are worthy of our kindly consideration. One of the benefits of a Christian civilization is that of an institution like the SPCA—the Society for the Prevention of Cruelty to Animals. To ill-treat a beast is to be devoid of the tenderness true humans possess. And a man who is unfeeling in his handling of an animal is usually destitute of the sympathy, love, and consideration for which some of his dear ones crave.

TWENTY-SEVENTH WEEK

THE LION FACE

JULY 2

...the face of a lion...
—Ezekiel 1:10; 10:14

The lion is the head of wild beasts, lord of the forest, and king of the jungle. Valor, courage, tenacity, strength, and determination are suggested by the wonderful face of a lion. (See Proverbs 30:30.) Isaiah uses the figure of the lion when he describes the lion-like courage of God. As a lion at bay, He refuses to surrender His own.

History records those who were known as "lions." Richard Cameron was described as "the lion of the Covenant." King Robert the Bruce was spoken of as being "brave as a lion." And the forces of sin, infidelity and apostasy demand that the righteous exhibit the boldness of a lion. May Spirit-inspired courage and tenacity be ours!

JULY 3

The Lion of the tribe of Judah.
—Revelation 5:5

As the lion was the ensign of the tribe of Judah, the figure is applied to Christ, Who sprang from that tribe, and Who manifested all the noble qualities of a lion. Satan, on the other hand, is like a lion at its worst. (See 1 Peter 5:8.) When up against Christ and His saints, the devil is ferocious in the extreme. One of his agents is likened unto a lion.

(See 2 Timothy 4:17.) Crouching subtle lions (see Deuteronomy 33:20; Genesis 49:9), however, hold no terror for courageous saints, who are well able to stop their mouth (see Hebrews 11:33). Daniel in the den of lions nerves many a hard pressed saint to fresh courage. (See Daniel 6:22; See Psalm 91:13.)

JULY 4

They were stronger than lions.
—2 Samuel 1:23

In David's beautiful eulogy of Saul and Jonathan, he described their daring, boldness, and strength as surpassing that of lion. Bold as lions (see Proverbs 28:1), we can yet be stronger than them. But wherein is a saint stronger than a lion? Well, the strength of a lion is natural, while our strength is supernatural. We are strengthened with all might by the Holy Spirit. Through Christ who strengthens us, we become braver and bolder than lions.

JULY 5

The slothful man saith, There is a lion without,
I shall be slain in the streets.
—Proverbs 22:13 (See also Proverbs 26:13.)

When dark, people in the East shut themselves in their house for fear of wild beasts. And Solomon, cognizant of this fact, uses it to prove how the indolent magnifies his difficulties, as an excuse for slothfulness. People who are kept busy are seldom pessimistic. With time on our hands, we brood over difficulties and although such could be overcome easily, cubs appear as fully grown, fierce lions. While we are active in service and prayer, lurking lions hold no dread for us. (See Psalm 22:21; 35:17.)

JULY 6

The young lions do lack, and suffer hunger.
—Psalm 34:10

Young lions are apt to starve, seeing that they are more or less dependent upon their parents. But the point of David, who knew a great deal about lions, and who often uses the figure of a lion, is that even the strongest may be smitten with hunger, but all who seek and serve the Lord shall not want any good thing. Of course, we must leave it to the Lord to decide what the good things are that we really need. A good many things for which we hunger are not good for us, and are wisely withheld.

JULY 7

He was unto me as...a lion in secret places.
—Lamentations 3:10

Jeremiah uses the lion in opposite ways. First of all, the prophet in his message on the broken covenant, depicts Israel as a lion turning and destroying its own. *"Mine heritage is unto me as a lion in the forest; it crieth out against me: therefore have I hated it"* (Jeremiah 12:8). In Lamentations, Jeremiah portrays God crouching as a lion waiting to spring upon its foes. And the rage of a lion is terrible. It never turns away for any. (See Proverbs 30:30; Amos 3:8.)

This is the day of grace. God is dealing with the multitudes in love. Woe be to the inhabitants on the earth when, in anger, He arises to mete out righteous judgment upon the godless! The wrath of the Lamb is to overtake those who reject His love and sacrifice.

JULY 8

The calf and the young lion...together;
and a little child shall lead them.
—Isaiah 11:6

The entrance of sin produced a change even in the nature of animals. Because of the voraciousness of many of the beasts, it is impossible for others to dwell near them. Calves cannot presently dwell with lions, unless it be within the lions! And as for a child leading a lion as a pet, what mother would trust her child within range of an uncaged lion?

But when Christ is on the earth, such is to be the quality of the millennium that even the animal creation is to be at peace. Wolves and lambs, calves and young lions will roam together and become the playthings of children. All fear is to be banished from the minds of men. And what a blissful era this will be for both man and beast!

TWENTY-EIGHTH WEEK

THE EAGLE FACE

JULY 9

...the face of an eagle.
—Ezekiel 1:10; 10:14

The eagle is supreme in the realm above, just as men, oxen, and lions, are supreme in their respective realms. Eagles have undisputed supremacy over the birds of the air. The eagle is king of the skies.

This kingly bird possesses a striking face. It carries nobility born of keenness of vision. High above the earth it is used to gazing into the vast expanse of heaven. What eyes the eagle has! Have we the eagle flight and face? A poet reminds us that "man at his best grows wings." Are we at our best? Have we developed wings? Alas, we fly too low! Our lives are too earthy. We fly according to the scale of the sparrow, hopping around the doors of the world for a few paltry crumbs. God means us to have the heavenly eyes of the eagle.

JULY 10

...as swift as the eagle flieth...
—Deuteronomy 28:49

None among the feathered creation can surpass the eagle in speed of flight. And interesting aspects of this fact are used by Jeremiah. (See Jeremiah 4:13; Lamentations 4:19.) Of all birds it is said to fly the highest, and with the greatest rapidity, and is thus used as a symbol of successive conquest. (See Jeremiah 48:40, 42; Hosea 8:1.) Its great swiftness is also used to describe the rapid flight of time. (See Job 9:26.) And its way in the air amazed Solomon (Proverbs 30:19).

Can we say we emulate the eagle here? Are we swift to obey? Like young Samuel, are we alive and quick to hear each murmur of God's voice?

JULY 11

As an eagle...so the LORD.
—Deuteronomy 32:11, 12

As a symbol of divine activities, the ways of an eagle are very expressive. (See Exodus 19:4; Jeremiah 48:40). In his song, Moses uses the eagle's tenderness and care of its young to describe beautifully God's kindness and provision. The stirring up of the nest, fluttering over the young, spreading abroad the wings, can all be applied to God's consideration of His own, and as a manifestation of grace to the sinner.

JULY 12

They shall mount up with wings as eagles.
—Isaiah 40:31

While the eagle mounts up and makes her nest on high at God's bidding (see Job 39:27), Isaiah, like David, saw in the eagle an emblem of renewed strength. Every year it molts, becoming almost naked and bald (see Micah 1:16) but appears to renew its youth with the appearances of a set of new feathers. *"Thy youth is renewed like the eagle's"* (Psalm 103:5).

And one day we are to have new feathers. At the return of the Lord, there will be a general molting. Seeing Him, we are to be like Him. And as He has the dew of His youth, our transformation into His likeness will mean the perpetuity of the strength of youthfulness.

JULY 13

Make thy nest as high as the eagle.
—Jeremiah 49:16

Many bird nests are robbed, simply because they are within easy reach. The eagle, however, has been endowed of God with wisdom (see Job 39:27), to build her nest on the highest crag of the rock, where she knows her eggs or young will be safe. But Jeremiah reminds Edom that her high and haughty spirit will be crushed. *"Though thou shouldst make thy nest as high as the eagle, I will bring thee down from thence, saith the LORD"* (Jeremiah 49:16). And, truly, He knows how to bring down the mighty from their seat.

JULY 14

A great eagle with great wings.
—Ezekiel 17:3, 7

Kings and kingdoms were symbolized by the eagle as Ezekiel's parable proves. The standards of the Roman army were eagles, and the same insignia is recognized by modern nations, to wit, America. The record of history, however, is that proud, imperial nations with eagle-like qualifies have a habit of disappearing. And masterful nations, presently gorging themselves with the spoil of smaller nations, as an eagle with carrion, will likewise perish. But the kingdom of the Lord endures forever.

JULY 15

They fly away as an eagle toward heaven.
—Proverbs 23:5

While Solomon had before his mind the power of earthly riches to vanish as if on wings, yet eagle flight heavenward has another application.

Because of the power and breadth of its wings it can soar nearer heaven than any other bird. It loves the heights. The glaring sun does not blind it. Have we this eagle trait? Do we love to fly toward heaven? Or can it be that we like to grovel among the mundane things of earth?

TWENTY-NINTH WEEK

DISCIPLES

JULY 16

Then are ye my disciples indeed.
—John 8:31

The word *"disciple"* means "a scholar," and it was thus that Jesus thought of those who turned to follow Him. *"Come unto me…and learn of me"* (Matthew 11:28–29) was His gracious invitation, and all who responded became scholars in the divine school. And that He found some of them dull, backward pupils, is apparent from a study of the gospels. But what patience the Teacher manifested! Are we in school with Christ? If so, what kind of scholars are we? Can we say that we are growing in grace and in knowledge?

JULY 17

Jesus shewed himself to his disciples.
—John 21:14

Disciples are indeed privileged to have the constant revelation of Jesus. Christless eyes see no beauty in Him that they should desire Him. And how can the spiritually blind discern His worth? But where there is an appreciation born of regeneration, Christ is ever ready to reveal the wonders of His Person and Word. Alone with Him, our hearts are thrilled with the lessons we learn. (See Mark 4:31.) Is He able constantly to reveal Himself to your waiting mind? Remember, it is only the pure in heart that can see Him.

JULY 18

And the disciples were called Christians first at Antioch.
—Acts 11:26

The sacred term *Christian* was used at Antioch as a nickname. Noticing how like Christ His disciples were, the name *Christian*, meaning a follower or slave of Christ, was coined. Followers of Wesley are known as *Wesleyans*. Disciples, then, are Christians, not only scholars, but saints. Learning of Christ, we become like Him. Unfortunately all disciples are not as *Christian* as they should be. Lessons are taken in the divine school, but the life of the Master-Teacher is not imbibed. The true purpose of our spiritual education is not the mere reception of knowledge from Him, but transformation into the Christ-likeness of life, which the designation of *Christian* implies.

JULY 19

All the disciples forsook him, and fled.
—Matthew 26:56

How disappointed Christ must be when disciples become deserters! By forsaking Jesus in the hour of need, the first disciples proved that they had not given strict attention to His word about taking up a cross and following Him. When the testing came, "the twelve" turned coward. Attachment, then, could not have been very deep. It is interesting to combine and contrast the two phases of the original disciples' experience with their Lord. And after three years of training in the school of the greatest Teacher ever, these selfsame men forsook Christ and fled. Can it be that you have deserted the Master? (Compare with John 6:66.)

JULY 20

He…began to wash the disciples' feet.
—John 13:5

One very hard lesson for the disciples to learn was that of humility. They wanted seats on a throne. Position was more important to them than hidden ministries. They were willing to shine, but not to serve. And so like the perfect Teacher He was, Jesus taught His own by example. In this pictorial fashion He inferred that the disciple is not above his master. (See Matthew 10:24.) Do you place honor before humility? Are you slow to learn from the teachings and example of your Lord that lowliness is the only road to lordship? The only way up is down.

JULY 21

Jesus ofttimes resorted thither with his disciples.
—John 18:2

A lovely garden makes a blessed prayer chamber. Surrounded with fragrant flowers, one draws near to God. Within the garden of Gethsemane was a sacred spot, so dear to Christ, to which He often retired with His own. And, as we read, Judas knew the place, and in his heartlessness made such a hallowed sanctuary the scene of his horrible surrender of Christ to His foes. Do you love to go into the garden of prayer with your Lord? Resorting thither with Him? Whether it be in a garden or a garret, are you truly one with the interceding Lord?

JULY 22

Art not thou also one of his disciples?
—John 18:25

Without doubt Peter was a disciple, yet in the sifting of Satan, he acted as if he were not one. He denied his association with Christ. "*Art not thou also one of His disciples? He denied it and said, I am not."* Proudly boasting that he was ready to go to prison or die for his Lord, he now disowns any allegiance to Him. Are you one of His disciples? If so, are you proud of the fact, or by lip and life are you denying the Master? Something about Peter indicated discipleship, for the world has a way of knowing if we have any association with Jesus.

THIRTIETH WEEK

WITNESSES

JULY 23

Ye shall be witnesses unto me.
—Acts 1:8

A true witness is one who sees and knows. (See Acts 26:16.) The apostles were thus competent witnesses of the things they recorded, because they saw and heard the things of which they spoke and wrote. They were likewise credible witnesses in that they had no interest to deceive, and suffered great hardship and even death, for the sake of their testimony.

As witnesses, we follow a goodly succession. The prophets of old are *"a cloud of witnesses"* (Hebrews 12:1) to the faithfulness of God. Christ is spoken of as *"the faithful witness"* (Revelation 1:5) because of faithfulness in declaring the truth of God, and sealing His testimony with His blood. *"The [Holy] Spirit itself beareth witness"* (Romans 8:16) by producing in us the graces of Christ.

JULY 24

Witnessing both to small and great.
—Acts 26:22

Paul was not crowd greedy. He lived too near the heart of his Master to neglect small audiences, for Jesus, we read, preached in *villages* as well as *cities*. Of course, Paul's determination to witness to small and great means that the position and prestige of men did not sway him. He was just as faithful among princes as among paupers. And yet we are warranted in making a further application. Paul was equally willing to address a few souls at the river side, as he was to preach to a crowd on Mars Hill.

You can always test a preacher's grace and pride by the way he reacts to small audiences or to invitations from inconspicuous spheres. Is your witness for small as well as great audiences?

JULY 25

Christ Jesus...witnessed a good confession.
—1 Timothy 6:13

As a faithful and true witness (see Revelation 1:5, 3:16; Isaiah 55:4), Jesus was unashamed of the truth, even in the presence of foes. He never compromised. And it was His reliability as a witness that greatly impressed Pilate and led him to work for the release of Christ. Are we witnessing a good confession? An effectual witness depends upon two things, namely, the life of the witness and the object of his witness. The life, death, resurrection, and teachings of Christ are what we have to witness to. (See Acts 1:8; 2:24; 3:15; 5:32; 10:39, 41; 13:31.) As to the life behind such a witness, it must be without spot, unrebukable until the return of Christ. (See 1 Timothy 6:13–14.)

JULY 26

A true witness delivereth souls.
—Proverbs 14:25

Solomon has some pointed things to say about witness-bearing in the chapter before us. "*A faithful witness will not lie; but a false witness will utter lies*" (verse 5). So there are two kinds of witnesses—faithful and false. The true witness delivers souls and never lies about the peril of rejecting Christ. The false witness deceives souls when the message he has to deliver is falsified. For instance, when a preacher tells a congregation that there is no eternal retribution for sin; that hell is not a grim reality, he lies, seeing that the express teaching of Christ affirms there is such a place of torment for all who despise His claims.

JULY 27

A witness, to bear witness of the Light.
—John 1:7

The ministry of John the Baptist was an enlightening one. Light came to men's minds as he testified of Christ, who came as *"the true Light"* (verse 9). Lest men should mistake the forerunner for the Fulfiller, John makes it clear that John the Baptist was not that light, but was sent to bear witness of that Light. And the purpose of such a witness was that "all men through him might believe."

Does our personal witness inspire faith? Have souls groping in the darkness of sin found their way to *"the light of the world,"* (John 8:12) as the result of our testimony? By lip and life are we bearing witness to the One whose precious blood can make the vilest sinner clean? As lights, let us not fail "the Light."

JULY 28

Ye receive not our witness.
—John 3:11

The ever-present tragedy in John's gospel is the rejection of Jesus by those He had come to bless. *"His own received him not"* (John 1:11). Is your loyal witness being spurned? Take courage! Here are the words of *"the faithful and true witness"* (Revelation 3:14): *"If I have told you of earthly things, and ye believe not, how shall ye believe, if I tell you of heavenly things?"* (John 3:12). Not always do those who listen to our earnest appeal, respond and believe. But how men react to our witness is not our responsibility. Our sacred task is to keep on witnessing.

JULY 29

Beheaded for the witness of Jesus...they lived and reigned.
—Revelation 20:4

What terrible deaths witnesses sometimes face! None testified so faithfully as Jesus, yet men gave Him a cruel cross. And this brings us back to the derivation of the word witnesses being related to "martyr." All honor to those who were willing to be beheaded for Christ's sake. John the Baptist lost his head. It was thus that young John and Betty Stain died at the hands of Chinese brigands. Some witnesses, alas, lose their heads, metaphorically speaking, in the wrong way. And yet, it is blessed to know that all who do die for Jesus, still live, and will yet reign, with the One for whom they suffered.

THIRTY-FIRST WEEK

BRANCHES

JULY 30

I am the vine, ye are the branches.
—John 15:5

A reliable resource, McClintock and Strong's *Cyclopaedia of Biblical, Theological, and Ecclesiastical Literature* (Volume 1), has it that "trees, in Scripture, denote great men and princes, and branches and plants denote their offspring. So Christ is the living Vine, and believers are the branches." And as branches are a vital part of the tree, derive their life from it, and bear its nature and fruit, in like manner, being in Christ, we derive our life from Him, and bear His nature. *"If the root be holy, so are the branches"* (Romans 11:16). As the branch cannot exist apart from the sap provided by the roots and trunk, so apart from Christ we are and can do nothing.

JULY 31

His branches shall spread.
—Hosea 14:6

Joseph is a fitting illustration of the spiritual prosperity of the believer, Hosea so beautifully portrays. *"Joseph is a fruitful bough, even a fruitful bough by a well; whose branches run over the wall"* (Genesis 49:22). A fruitful bough by a well! As the "well" is a fitting type of the Holy Spirit (see John 4:14), we here have the secret of fruitfulness. The Spirit is the sap—making our fruit and multiplied usefulness possible. And when fully possessed by the Spirit our branches spread in every direction. They run over all the walls of our church, denomination, or community. How far does your branch spread? (See Psalm 80:11.)

AUGUST 1

The branch of the Lord *be beautiful and glorious.*
—Isaiah 4:2

As a name of Christ, Branch is used in various ways (Isaiah 11:1; Jeremiah 23:5; 33:15; Zechariah 3:8; 6:12). As He is rightly named the Branch, upon Him hang the unspeakable blessings of pardon, peace, hope, and heaven. And that such a term can be applied to Israel and to the church is evident from Psalm 80:15. The Lord Jesus Christ as *"the branch"* was and is both beautiful and glorious. Man-ward, He was beautiful in life and character. How great is Thy beauty! Godward, He was glorious, glorifying the Father in all His words, works, and ways. He was in turn glorified of the Father. And now we see Jesus crowned with glory. Are the beauty and glory of the Lord discernible in your life and mine?

AUGUST 2

Every branch in me that beareth not fruit he taketh away.
—John 15:2

Here is a phrase that has caused no little concern. Does it teach that we can be saved today and lost tomorrow? Certainly not! First of all, notice where the believer as a branch is—in Me. And once one is an integral part of Christ, such a union can never be dissolved. Communion may be severed, but *union—never.* The words *"taketh away"* can be translated "lifted up." A gardener, noticing a branch trailing in the dust, where it cannot enjoy the sun and the full benefit of nature's forces, lifts it up, gives it a higher position. Often fruit is not ours because our living, as branches, is too near the earth. So the divine Gardener comes along and raises us up from worldly desires. Is your branch high enough?

AUGUST 3

The dew lay all night upon my branch.
—Job 29:19

In his parable, part of which we have in this chapter, Job gives us a glimpse into his past life of affluence and influence. But now, stripped bare, he recalls the abundant riches he once possessed. Now that he is destitute, he thinks of himself as a withered tree. The day was, however, when his roots went down to the waters, and the night dew produced continual fruit. *"Dew"* is a fitting type of the Holy Spirit's silent, beneficial ministry. The question is: How does the night of sorrow affect you as a branch? Do the withering influences of adversity and trial leave you untouched, because of the continual falling of the heavenly Dew upon the branch?

AUGUST 4

Branch of my planting…that I may be glorified.
—Isaiah 60:21

If we have been planted by a divine hand, then no one and nothing can unplant us. *"Every plant, which my heavenly Father hath not planted, shall be rooted up"* (Matthew 15:13; see also John 10:28–29). Therefore, God will not suffer demons or men to undo the work of His hands. A further thought is that He carefully prunes and nourishes His branches in order that their fruit might glorify His name. (See John 15:5, 8.) Alas, some of us carry more leaves of profession than fruit of practice. A vine-dresser, however, knows that all his work on the vine is justified, once the luscious grapes appear.

AUGUST 5

As the branch cannot bear fruit of itself, except it abide in the vine.
—John 15:4

Hosea's lament was that Israel was *"an empty vine he bringeth forth fruit unto himself"* (John 10:1) and that such fruit was *"the fruit of lies"* (verse 13). The true source of fruit is referred to later on in the book, *"From me is thy fruit found"* (John 14:8). It is not the responsibility of a branch to produce fruit. All it can do is to bear the fruit, the continual supply of sap from the tree makes possible. A good deal of so-called *"fruit"* in Christian service is self-produced. In Galatians 5, Paul is careful to distinguish between *"works of the flesh"* (verse 19) and *"the fruit of the Spirit"* (verse 22).

THIRTY-SECOND WEEK

SOLDIERS

AUGUST 6

A good soldier of Jesus Christ.
—2 Timothy 2:3

Paul's life in prison, where he was continually chained to a soldier, supplied him with a fertile field of illustration. This is why military metaphors abound in his writings. And a collection of these striking metaphors of Christian life and service makes a forceful Bible reading. Paul called Epaphroditus a *"fellowsoldier"* (Philippians 2:25). The apostle, therefore, looked upon ministers as soldiers, on account of the hardships and difficulties to which they are exposed as they faithfully preach Christ. And as soldiers, we are not to whine when privations and difficulties come our way. As soldiers of the cross we must not expect to be carried to the skies on flowery beds of ease.

AUGUST 7

That he may please him who hath chosen him to be a soldier.
—2 Timothy 2:4

In this war-torn world of ours, men are conscripted as soldiers. But the divine Captain has no conscripts. It is all voluntary enlistment in His army. And when a soldier dons his uniform he has to say "fare-well" to a good many legitimate affairs of life such as home, business, pleasure, politics. His supreme task, as a soldier, is the defense of his country. And it is only as he is un-entangled that he can fight. We have been chosen to war against the world, flesh, and Satan. Victories, however, will only come our way as we strip ourselves of all that is not only unclean, but unnecessary.

AUGUST 8

The soldiers…took his garments.
—John 19:23

In their gamble for the clothes of Christ, the soldiers preserved His coat intact. To tear it in four would destroy it. The soldier winning the toss carried off the seamless robe and doubtless wore it with pride, as a trophy of plunder. But wearing Christ's coat did not make him Christ's. Arrayed in such a well-spun coat, the soldier would look somewhat like Christ, yet he was far from being a Christian. And how many men there are who look like Christ. They wear His clothes; they pray, read the Bible, go to church, and perform Christian deeds: yet they have never been truly born again.

AUGUST 9

A devout soldier…that waited on him continually.
—Acts 10:7

Cornelius must have valued the faithful service of the soldier. Evidently, he had reverence, for he was "*devout.*" And a man, even as a soldier in his nation's army, should be a better, brave soldier if he has first of all sworn allegiance to Jesus Christ. Then the soldier of Cornelius waited upon his master continually. He was at his beck and call. He had long learned that a soldier's first and constant duty is obedience. Can we say that as soldiers of Christ we are devout and obedient?

AUGUST 10

They gave large money unto the soldiers.
—Matthew 28:12

The bribe of large money was a great temptation to the Roman soldiers guarding the tomb of Jesus. And, in taking the money and circulating the lie about Christ's body having been stolen by His disciples, they disgraced their uniform and profession as soldiers. The pity is that they were bought over by religion leaders. Large money! It is sometimes the snare of the Christian soldier. Often the cause of Christ is hurt by the insistence of well-known evangelists and teachers for large, guaranteed sums ere their service is rendered. A man prostitutes his gift when he fails to scatter it freely, depending upon God to bring him all that is necessary for his needs.

AUGUST 11

Who goeth a warfare any time at his own charges?
—1 Corinthians 9:7

Once a man enlists and finds himself a soldier, all care as to raiment and food ceases. The nation undertakes to look after him, and likewise carry the responsibility of his dependents, so that he can be free to fight the country's battles. Those who enter the army, live of the army. Thus is it with those who are called to preach the gospel. (See verse 14.) Whom God calls, He cares for! All necessary provision is promised. Our divine Captain knows all that we must have for ourselves and our dear ones. Soldiers do not worry about their food and raiment and allowances for wives and children. They let their country do the worrying. Would that we could learn to leave all our needs with Him Who has called us to serve Him!

AUGUST 12

The weapons of our warfare are not carnal,
but mighty through God.
—2 Corinthians 10:4

Chained, as he was, to a soldier during his imprisonment, Paul had ample time to study the ways of soldiers. And it is this fact, as we have already noted, that accounts for the apostle's military phraseology. The duties, uniform, weapons, and habits of Roman soldiers were carefully observed and given a spiritual application. Thus, all the necessary accoutrements for Christian warfare are indicated. Our mighty spiritual weapons—armor, sword and shield are given attention. (See Ephesians 6:11–18.) What we fail to remember, however, is the truth that the Lord's battles can only be fought with the Lord's weapons.

THIRTY-THIRD WEEK

OUR LIVES

AUGUST 13

The son of man is not come to destroy men's lives.
—Luke 9:56

On our nationally recognized Labor Day, a great deal will be said and written regarding the dignity and doings of labor. The fact remains, however, that much produced by labor destroys men's lives. Science and labor are combined to kill the greatest number of men in the shortest possible time. Christianity, on the other hand, is a life-saver. Christ certainly destroys those forces responsible for men's departure from God, but He ever strives to save, not only the soul, but the life. Are you helping Christ in His glorious work of saving lives?

AUGUST 14

They made their lives bitter with hard bondage.
—Exodus 1:14

The Egyptians grievously oppressed the Israelites. Under Pharaoh, life became well-nigh intolerable. It was so for the church in the days of Nero. And as we think of Europe with its terrible concentration camps, we realize that dictatorships are making lives of multitudes of God-fearing souls bitter with hard bondage. But the heavenly Moses is at hand to deliver His own from cruel servitude. And persecuted saints can afford to wait. The day is coming! As persecuted Israel has stood by the grave of many a Pharaoh, so saints, killed all the daylong for Christ's sake, will yet witness the overthrow of those satanic agencies responsible for present hardship.

AUGUST 15

A people that jeopardized their lives.
—Judges 5:18

Men that have hazarded their lives.
—Acts 15:26

We bracket these phrases together, seeing that Zebulun at Naphtali, Barnabas and Paul, were alike in their prodigal expenditure of life. If, for the sake of science, discovery, and adventure, men are willing to risk their lives, surely those of us who are followers of Christ, Who, for our sakes, was willing to jeopardize His life unto the death, will not come behind the surrender of the world? May the Lord grant a little more sanctified daring and audacity in our witness! Charging the devil "*in the high places of the field,*" (Judges 5:18), may we count it a privilege to be numbered with those who love not their lives unto death.

AUGUST 16

Lovely and pleasant in their lives.
—2 Samuel 1:23

David's eulogy of Saul and Jonathan is one of the world literary masterpieces. A close association with father and son led the psalmist to extol the beautiful and unique companionship that had existed between the two. Would that the same description were true of us all! How is it that we have many charming sinners and far too many sour saints in the world? Grace ought to make us gracious. If pardoned, we ought to be pleasant! Loveliness and pleasantness cannot be artificially produced. They are the outcome of unbroken fellowship with our charming Lord. And redeemed men and women should ever be a delightsome people.

AUGUST 17

We ought to lay down our lives for the brethren.
—1 John 3:16

It is not a mere coincidence that John 3:16 and 1 John 3:16 are both related to sacrifice of life on behalf of others. Both are Calvary verses. In the latter verse, however, John brings us to the claim the cross has upon our lives. Christ laid down His life for us and, in turn, we must be willing to lay down our lives for others. But can we say that we have reached the Calvary ideal? Are we prepared to die for our brothers and sisters in Christ? Die for the brethren! God knows, we often kill the brethren with our jealousy, ill will, backbiting, and slander.

AUGUST 18

This voyage will be with hurt and much damage...of our lives.
—Acts 27:10

A fitting caption for this dramatic chapter would be, "A Saint in a Storm." Storms often prove the depth of saintliness. In Paul's perilous voyage to Rome we have the exhibition of his moral and spiritual ascendency. Amid panic he was peaceful. Sensing imminent danger, he warns of damage to human cargo. And the Christian life is akin to a voyage. We ourselves are as ships that pass in the night, and sailing is dangerous. The storms we encounter hurt and damage the body. Ultimately, however, we are to make port, even although it will be with tattered sails. Our Pilot, who is on board, will see to our safe landing.

AUGUST 19

Nor angels...shall be able to separate us from the love of God.
—Romans 8:38–39

That angels have enormous, relegated power is seen in the work of the angel who smote 185,000 Assyrians. Peter speaks of angels as being *"greater in might and power"* (2 Peter 2:11) than proud, evil men. Yet so indissoluble is the bond between Christ and His own that an archangel or angel is not able to break it. In Christ we are eternally secure. No force, heavenly, human, or hellish can divide the Savior and the saved. Hallelujah!

THIRTY-FOURTH WEEK

OUR HOMES

AUGUST 20

Bring these men home.
—Genesis 43:16

Here we have the first reference to *"home"* in the Bible. *"House,"* meaning, of course, all Noah's loved ones and possessions, occurs for the first time in Genesis 7:1. Joseph would feel very much at home as all his brothers gathered around the table. And is it not the desire of our heavenly Joseph to bring us all home? Christ's great *"at home"* day is not far away. Presently, we are *"at home in the body"* (2 Corinthians 5:6). Ere long, reunion above will be ours, just as Joseph was happy to have his own around him in his Egyptian home.

AUGUST 21

Man goeth to his long home.
—Ecclesiastes 12:5

What constitutes a true, earthly home? Not riches nor culture, but love, harmony, and the recognition of Jesus Christ as Savior and Lord. An old song has it, "There is beauty all around, when there's love at home." And heaven is a blessed expansion and extension of a godly home life. Jesus referred to heaven as "the Father's home" as Westcott and Hort translate John 14:3. Is it not comforting to know that the

Great Beyond is our *"long home"* (Ecclesiastes 12:5)? Precious home life on earth is ruptured by death. Home life above is eternal.

AUGUST 22

Abroad the sword bereaveth, at home there is as death.
—Lamentations 1:20

Ezekiel speaks of *"the sword is without, and the pestilence and the famine within"* (Ezekiel 7:15). How up to date is the prophet's description? In the almost total war the earth is experiencing, the sword is active, bereaving hearts and homes, while at home pestilences famines, fear, distress, and shock claim untold numbers. At home there is death! Has death shadowed your little home? Do you gaze at a vacant chair, and listen in vain for the familiar step? Well, may you learn that often Jesus permits our home to be emptied, so that in the place of the one He takes, He may give us more of Himself.

AUGUST 23

Ye brought it home, I did blow upon it.
—Haggai 1:9

The Lord had some caustic things to say about the people who could spend plenty on their lovely homes, but who were content with a shack of a place for the worship of His name. Judgment, however, came upon those who prided themselves upon their ceiled houses. The Lord blew upon their coveted possessions. What have you brought home? Do you feel proud of costly furniture, rugs, pictures, antiques, and rare editions? Have you spent more on these than on God? Does your home receive the worship God should have? Then beware, lest He blow upon your home gods.

AUGUST 24

Let me first go...home.
—Luke 9:61

Our Lord knew that if the man desiring to follow Him returned home to bid farewell that he would remain home. The home pull would prove to be too strong, and He would lose a good disciple. And what judgment rests upon a home in which yearnings in the breast of one with it is forcibly restricted? It was a different kind of home Jesus sent His mother to. In response to the dying wish of Christ, John took Mary into his own home. Can the Master, with any confidence, send anyone to your home to be helped and cared for?

AUGUST 25

Go home to thy friends, and tell them how great things
the Lord hath done for thee.
—Mark 5:19

The maniac of Gadara, after his wonderful deliverance from demonism, wanted to remain with Christ and publicly serve Him. But the Master knew that his witness would be more effective in his own home and home town. And home he went, to declare the great things Christ had done for him; and, as we read, all men marveled. Some of us have no hesitation in facing crowds. It is not quite so easy to speak to our own dear ones about Christ. Home can become the most difficult sphere in which to testify. If silence and timidity are yours, let the Lord embolden you as you determine to *"go home...and tell."*

AUGUST 26

Shew piety at home.
—1 Timothy 5:4 (See also Titus 2:5.)

Home saints and home keepers are all too rare. What hypocrisy it is to be pious in church, to pray like a saint on a Sunday, and then fight like a demon at home on Monday! Do you add to the joy and sacredness of your home? Have you have sanctity devoid of sanctimoniousness that makes your home life so precious and attractive? Further, is it not dishonoring to the Lord when home ties and responsibilities are neglected even for Christian service? A dirty house and neglected children militate against the influences of parents who run to every meeting. A fragrant home life and parenthood often involve the sacrifice of a good deal of public service.

THIRTY-FIFTH WEEK

OUR MONEY

AUGUST 27

Ye shall be redeemed without money.
—Isaiah 52:3 (See also Isaiah 55:1.)

Money speaks! Well, it may, but money cannot save. Gold is able to buy almost anything of value. When it comes to the redemption of the soul, however, not a cent is required. The rich and the poor must meet together and tread the same road leading to the Crucified. And yet, while it is true that our money cannot redeem us, once we are saved, the Lord desires our dedicated substance in order that He may reach others. Saved, we are, without money and without price. But we cannot serve the Savior without money and without price.

AUGUST 28

He that loveth silver shall not be satisfied.
—Ecclesiastes 5:10

The more a rich man has, the more he wants. If he sets out to amass fifty thousand dollars, reaching his objective, he wants another fifty thousand dollars to keep the first company. It is always dissatisfying to love silver for silver's sake. Not money, but the love of it is the root of all evil. It was here that Judas erred. Are you satisfied with what you have, whether it is much or little? Or can it be that your love for silver has destroyed your love for the Savior?

AUGUST 29

Thy silver and thy gold is mine.
—1 Kings 20:3

Thy—MINE! What we call our own is not ours, but His! There are those who hoard their dollars as if they had the exclusive use of such. Often money is saved or spent without any reference to God's will regarding its disposal. If His, then He has a definite claim upon all we are and have. And there would be plenty of support for the Lord's work at home and abroad if only the Lord's people believed that their substance was the Lord's money. Has God free access to all your silver and gold? Can you sing, "Not a mite would I withhold?" (Frances Ridley Havergal, "Take My Life").

AUGUST 30

The street of the city was pure gold.
—Revelation 21:21

America has piles of gold stored away. The wealth of some eighty per cent of the world's nations has found its way here for safety and exchange. And the precious ore is closely guarded because of its intrinsic value. The values of earth, however, are not recognized in heaven. Gold there is used as road metal. What men covet down here helps to pave the streets above. Here we worship gold, in heaven we are to walk on it. How slow we are to learn that our attitude towards money is a true indication of character. What he gathers it for, and how he uses it, stamps the owner as miserly or liberal-hearted.

AUGUST 31

Put my money to the exchangers.
—Matthew 25:27

Wherefore then gavest not thou my money into the bank…?
—Luke 19:23

It is clearly evident from our Lord's teaching that there is a legitimate trading of money. A man is no less a saint because of a wise investment of his money. He will, of course, be careful where he invests, and of how he uses the interest accruing. Alas, many a Christian, fascinated by high and quick returns offered by unreliable companies, has lost precious money the Lord could have used for the evangelization of lost souls. A safe policy to pursue is that laid down by John Wesley: "Get all you can; save all you can; give all you can."

SEPTEMBER 1

Having land, sold it, and brought the money,
and laid it at the apostles' feet.
—Acts 4:37

There is something fascinating about the Pentecostal communism of the early church. "*Neither said any of them that ought of the things which he possessed was his own; but they had all things common*" (Acts 4:32). Lands and houses were sold and the money laid at the feet of the apostles for distribution as every man had need. Ananias and Sapphira were suddenly destroyed because of their partial surrender. Professedly, their all was on the altar, but they kept back part of the price. Do you delight in bringing your money and, laying it at the feet of Jesus, ask Him for wisdom in the disposal of it?

SEPTEMBER 2

They that received tribute money came to Peter, and said,
Doth not your master pay tribute?
—Matthew 17:24

If rates and taxes do claim a somewhat large part of our income, it is somewhat encouraging to learn that the Master willingly paid tribute. He met every just demand. Rather than evade the tax-collector, He performed a miracle to provide sufficient tribute money for Himself and His own.

The finding of the silver is sometimes used in another connection. Burdened by schemes for money-raising, the church forgets that if only she will go out after the fish, she will find all the money she needs in the mouth of those caught. A church, strong on evangelism, has few financial problems.

THIRTY-SIXTH WEEK

OUR TALENTS

SEPTEMBER 3

Unto one he gave five talents, to another two, and to another, one.
—Matthew 25:15

By the *"talents,"* we are to understand those natural and spiritual gifts God graciously bestows upon men. And while any gift can and must be developed, we must ever be careful to trace all gifts to the divine Source. Further, talents are to be traded with. Whatever gift or gifts we have received, by use they are multiplied. It may be that your complaint is that you are not talented? The fact remains, however, that every Christian has some gift or another to exercise. *"To every man according to his several ability."* Discover your talent and trade with it. Let the latent become patent!

SEPTEMBER 4

I was afraid, and went and hid thy talent.
—Matthew 25:25

Solomon reminds us of the *"sore evil...riches kept for the owners thereof to their hurt"* (Ecclesiastes 5:13). And severe condemnation overtook the one-talent man for keeping his gift to himself. Suffering from an inferiority complex, he was afraid to use the little he had. Instead of bartering with his talent, he buried it. He was meant to trade with it on the earth, but hid it in the earth instead. The principle, therefore, enunciated by the Master in His parable is "Use it or lose it!" Is fear causing you to hide your talent? Out with it, and employ it to the full! The man with the one talent would have received the same commendation as the man with five, had he been equally faithful. Let this encourage you to serve Christ to the utmost of your ability.

SEPTEMBER 5

One was brought unto him, which owed him ten thousand talents.
—Matthew 18:24

How deep in debt we are! We owe God and man more than we can ever pay. Our tragedy, however, is the failure to pay what we are able. Paul realized that he was a debtor, and while he knew that he could never pay back all he owed to Christ, yet thinking of the need of all men, he unceasingly labored to discharge his debt. All his faculties were employed to the limit for the highest welfare of saint and sinner alike. *"Pay me that thou owest"* (verse 28) has more than one application.

SEPTEMBER 6

Lord, behold, here is they pound,
which I have kept laid up in a napkin.
—Luke 19:20

The servant in our Lord's parable of the nobleman was guilty of a twofold error when he hid his pound in a napkin. First of all, he failed to use the pound to good purpose. He covered it, instead of circulating it. Then he erred, in that he wrapped the money in a napkin of face cloth. The very handkerchief that should have been used to wipe the sweat from his brow as he legitimately traded with the pound was likewise perverted from its intended ministry. Thus the wrong use of one gift inevitably leads to the misuse of another.

SEPTEMBER 7

Serve him with a perfect heart and with a willing mind.
—1 Chronicles 28:9

The mind is a God-given faculty we cannot afford to neglect. Power to think and understand distinguishes men from beasts. But our minds can only function to the full as they are instructed by *"the mind of Christ"* (1 Corinthians 2:16). Thus controlled, they have the *"readiness of mind"* (Acts 17:11) to search the Scriptures daily and *"the humility of mind"* (Acts 20:19) with which to serve the Lord. On the other hand, those abandoned by God are characterized by *"a reprobate mind"* (Romans 1:28).

SEPTEMBER 8

Sound speech, that cannot be condemned…
—Titus 2:8

The gift of speech, while it may prove to be dangerous, if not always seasoned with grace, is yet another talent we can use with great profit. The words of our mouth, whether in conversation or ministry, must ever be acceptable to God. Happy is the man who, talented as a speaker, can confess, *"My speech shall distil as the dew, as the small rain upon the tender herb, and as the shadows upon the grass"* (Deuteronomy 32:2). Christ controlled lips always produce an excellency of speech, commendable of Him of Whom men said, *"Never man spake like this man"* (John 7:46).

SEPTEMBER 9

I live; yet not I…
—Galatians 2:20

Personality is also to be numbered among the talents with which we can trade. Before his conversion, Paul must have had a strong conspicuous personality. And now, as a Christian, the apostle is still conscious of this endowment. *"I live."* Grace, then, did not destroy his personality, but dominated it. It became harmonized with another Personality. *"I live; yet not I...Christ liveth in me."* Have you this subtle gift of personality? If so, how do you use it? Do you so employ it as to draw men and women to yourself, or do you use it to draw others to your Lord.

THIRTY-SEVENTH WEEK

THE GLORY OF GOD

SEPTEMBER 10

Glorify your Father which is in heaven.
—Matthew 5:16

If we would be virtuous in life and fruitful in service, the glory of God must be the center and circumference of all our desires and doings. The song of the angels, *"Glory to God in the highest"* (Luke 2:14) was quickly learned by the shepherds, who heard it, for they returned home *"glorifying and praising God"* (verse 20). Jesus could confess that He had glorified the Father on the earth. Can we say that a consuming passion burns within our hearts to see God magnified? It is sadly possible to glory in our gifts, our church, our denomination, and for these aspects to detract from the glory of God. (See Proverbs 25:27.) Self-glory, however, is shallow glory. *"The glory of Jacob shall be made thin"* (Isaiah 17:4).

SEPTEMBER 11

She was made straight, and glorified God.
—Luke 13:13

It would seem as if some professed Christians are slow to learn that they must be straight in all their transactions if their witness is to glorify God. Like the woman loosed from her infirmity, we, too, must first of all be made straight, and then with an adjusted life, bring glory to God. Paul reminds us that by our eating, drinking, and our every action it is possible to glorify God. (See 1 Corinthians 10:31; 1 Peter 4:11.) Whatsoever ye do! Surely, such a command covers a wide range. Are we a little crooked in what we do? Can it be that our life in some aspect or other is not quite upright? Well, the Lord is able to straighten us out, and contribute, thereby, to His own glory.

SEPTEMBER 12

They glorified him not as God.
—Romans 1:21

Three distinguishing features of heathenism and of Gentile world apostasy are ignorance of God, contempt of God and neglect of God. They knew not—glorified not—neither were thankful. Alas, we, too, can be guilty of apostate contempt of God! Professing to believe in God, we easily yield to fear and anxiety as we face the trials and needs of life. We act as if He were not almighty enough to carry all our burdens and deliver us out of all our distresses. Though weak in faith, we glorify Him not as God. (See Daniel 5:23; Acts 12:23.)

SEPTEMBER 13

Wherefore glorify ye the LORD *in the fires.*
—Isaiah 24:15

As Chrysostom was being led out to exile, he exultantly cried, "Glory to God for all events!" And many a martyr has been inspired to glorify God as literal fires consumed them. How do we act in the fires? When trial, disappointment, adversity and persecution surround us do we, as Christians, *"glorify God on this behalf"* (1 Peter 4:16)? To offer praise, not only for the things we like, but for the things that hurt, is to magnify Him whose *"grace is ever sufficient"* (Psalm 50:23). And that the fiery furnace of affliction can be fashioned into a powerful pulpit is evidenced by the record of Paul, who could glory even in his infirmities and tribulations.

SEPTEMBER 14

Glorify God in your body.
—1 Corinthians 6:20

As the temple of the Holy Spirit, the body is indeed a sacred shrine in which everything should speak of God's glory. Bodily appetites, actions and functions must be Spirit controlled. The enormous size of some bodies indicates indulgence at the table; while the way in which others are decked with artificial beauty, or, on the other hand, almost destitute of proper clothing, reveal ignorance as to what God requires of the body. Horace Bushnell has said, "It is possible to dress in the Spirit." Indeed, all associated with the body should reveal the Lord Who dwells within. Thresholds and gateways to the body, no less than the shrine within, should be holy ground, rare, unearthly, and strange.

SEPTEMBER 15

I have given unto them the words which thou gavest me.
—John 17:8

Our Lord in this assertion reminds His Father in His high-priestly prayer that the truth He declared was not *conceived* within His own mind, but *received* from God. And this means that Christ was not an original preacher. The words given Him by the Father were, in turn, transmitted to His own.

And we are certainly not in the world to give the multitudes our thoughts, ideas, or speculations regarding the Bible, but the Bible itself. Preach the Word! There is no better way of glorifying the Lord.

SEPTEMBER 16

He gave not God the glory.
—Acts 12:23

The praise of man turned Herod's head. After his eloquent oration, the people shouted, *"It is the voice of a god, and not of a man"* (Acts 12:22). But because God cannot give His glory to another, He immediately smote Herod. And to add to the humiliation of one eaten up of pride, he was eaten up of worms. Alas, the plaudits of a crowd seldom generate humility! Speakers and singers are sorely tempted to become proud and conceited. If we have any measure of platform gift, let us ever be careful to give God the glory seeing He is jealous of His own Person.

THIRTY-EIGHTH WEEK

THE LOVE OF CHRIST

SEPTEMBER 17

The love of Christ, which passeth knowledge.
—Ephesians 3:19

Paul makes it clear in his prayer for inner fullness and knowledge, that to know the unknowable love of Christ one must be rooted and grounded in love. To be able to comprehend the breadth, length, depth and height of the love of Him, whose love surpasses that of a woman's, one must have a heart saturated with such a divine love. To know the love of Christ, we must first know the Christ of love. And, further, the knowledge the apostle refers to is not a mere mental understanding of the love in question, but an experimental knowledge. It is a knowledge born of faith. And such a love is both of the head and the heart.

SEPTEMBER 18

The love of Christ constraineth us.
—2 Corinthians 5:14

The impelling motive in all effective service is the love of Christ and love *to* Christ. Paul never journeys very far from this double incentive. Constrained by love! How this destroys all ulterior motives in ministry! Love of self, love of crowds, love of applause, love of money—all lesser loves are consumed by the mastering love of Christ. Further down in this chapter Paul speaks of beseeching men to be reconciled to God.

And he could beseech them in Christ's stead, seeing he had a heart constantly warmed by the love of Him he dearly loved.

SEPTEMBER 19

He first loved us.
—1 John 4:19

For an inner understanding of divine love we have to live near the writings of John, the Apostle of Love. There, before us, is the truth of God's initiative in love. Herein is love, yes, the most fascinating form of love; not that we loved God, for the natural mind is at enmity with God, but that in our wicked and rebellious condition, He loved us and manifested His love in the sacrifice of the cross. (See Ephesians 2:4.) In His love and in His pity He redeemed us. John further teaches *us* that we must emulate the divine example, and take the first step in loving the unloving and unlovable. If we would be perfect in love, our hearts must go out to lost souls irrespective of their condition and position.

SEPTEMBER 20

Having loved his own…he loved them unto the end.
—John 13:1

A more effective translation would be "He loved them to the uttermost." So we have an uttermost love as well as an uttermost salvation. And the latter is the product of the former. It is not a mere coincidence that the conception of Judas' dark crime immediately follows. Christ loved the traitor to the end. Love must have striven to prevent Judas betraying the Master, but failed. Is it not blessed to know that, even although we disappoint Jesus, He never casts us off? His is the love that will not let us go. It is not a love continuous upon human merit and response.

SEPTEMBER 21

...one of his disciples, whom Jesus loved.
—John 13:23 (See also John 11:5.)

At the moment, I am sitting beneath a blazing sun in Florida, and the thought has just come to me that although the sun is for the world, and its beneficial rays are for all mankind, yet here am I, allowing it to expend its fullness on me. The sun is for all, and yet for each. Thus it is with the love of Christ. Along with the Father, He loves the world. The miracle of grace, however, is the fact that He focuses His love on me. In that Bethany home Jesus was fond of visiting, there were three persons so distinct in personal traits, yet each was loved by Christ. Are you not amazed at Christ's loving *you?*

SEPTEMBER 22

Conquerors through him that loved us.
—Romans 8:37

Love liberates! In his doxology, John also emphasizes the emancipating power of love *"Unto Him that loved us, and washed us from our sins"* (Revelation 1:5). Paul, of course, links love to deliverance from injury, John, from iniquity. And we can be certain that the love freeing us from sin, will see to our freedom from the sword and slaughter men would employ to separate us from the Savior. Once we clasp the hand of love divine, no one and nothing can ever separate us from the love of God which is in Christ Jesus our Lord.

SEPTEMBER 23

Walk in love, as Christ also hath loved us.
—Ephesians 5:2

Paul was ever practical in his application of the truth. If we are the Lord's, it is incumbent upon us to live a life of love. Among ourselves as Christians, there must be the constant display of that love generated by the Holy Spirit. (See 1 Peter 1:22.) Walk in love! How do we walk? Why, we use two feet and take one step at a time. Well, the two feet of love are before us in this chapter, namely, love in the church and love in the home. Saints are to love one another, and husbands have to love their wives. (See Ephesians 5:25.) And to walk in love means to leave behind us the footprints of love.

THIRTY-NINTH WEEK

THE JUDGMENT SEAT

SEPTEMBER 24

We shall all stand before the judgment seat of Christ.
—Romans 14:10

That this particular judgment is exclusively for believers can be proven by turning back to verse eight: *"we are the Lord's."* And what a powerful incentive to life and service is the thought that we must appear at the tribunal to render an account of our stewardship! The immediate association, however, Paul offers is that of our present judgment of a brother in Christ, and of His judgment of us all when we gather around Him. We are not to spend our time judging one another. If a brother is happy in what he allows, even though his allowance is contrary to our standards, we are to wait for the Judgment Seat to bring its condemnation. (See Romans 14:12–23.)

SEPTEMBER 25

We must all appear before the judgment seat of Christ.
—2 Corinthians 5:10

The apostle Paul labored that he might be accepted of Christ. The approval of men mattered little. What he lived for was his Master's *"Well done"* (Matthew 25:21). But the connection here is that of the judgment of Christ upon the believer's acts, whether good or bad. As there is a tendency to think of the Bema as being wholly connected with rewards, it is as well to emphasize the necessary adjustments that must be made as the Judge is faced. Every work, every secret thing, whether good or evil must be brought into judgment. (See Ecclesiastes 11:9; 12:14.) If our deeds are bad, loss will be ours, not of heaven, but of a position in coming glory. The wood, hay, stubble will be consumed. (See 1 Corinthians 3:12–15.) Let us endeavor to get rid of the bad while on this side of eternity.

SEPTEMBER 26

[God] hath given him authority to execute judgment.
—John 5:27

While it is apparent from John 5:24 and 3:18 that present condemnatory judgment cannot be applied to the believers, yet a judgment does await him, and that the One responsible for his salvation is likewise to judge his service. As the Son of God and the Son of Man, He will examine us in the light of divine and human standards. And of this we can be confident, that He will execute righteous judgment. (See Revelation 16:7; 19:2.) Favoritism will not characterize any of His decisions. Every one of us will receive the due reward of our deeds.

SEPTEMBER 27

I will give thee a crown of life.
—Revelation 2:10

How relieved we are to know that the text reads, "Be thou faithful," and not "Be thou successful"! Some are faithful but not very successful, as the world counts success. On the other hand, there are those who are successful, but not very faithful in the means used to attain success. Faithfulness is to be the basis of reward at the Judgment Seat. Well done, good and faithful servant! Our crown depends upon our fidelity, not our fame; upon our sincerity, not our success; upon the quality of our work, and not the quantity of it.

SEPTEMBER 28

Who without respect of persons
judgeth according to every man's work.
—1 Peter 1:17

As the Father *"judgeth righteously"* (1 Peter 2:23) so will the Master weigh every case on its own merits at the Judgment Seat. Wealth and influence are able to sway the decisions of human judges. And nothing is so disastrous to our social and national life as perverted justice. Respect of persons, however, will not be tolerated by our Lord. Whether it be a dear, old washer-woman, unknown by the world, or the renowned preacher lauded by the multitudes, each will have his labor tried by fire, of what sort it is. And what reversals this judgment will witness! Then, some of the presently conspicuous, because of their gifts and possessions, will be humiliated.

SEPTEMBER 29

What is our...crown of rejoicing?
—1 Thessalonians 2:19

Motivated by the thought that souls saved through his instrumentality would arise to greet him at the Judgment Seat, Paul gave himself, without reserve, to the ingathering of the lost. His hope, glory, joy, crown of rejoicing, as he stands in the presence of his Lord, are the Thessalonians he was used to save. Are there those who will shine as stars in our crown? Is ours to be the joy of having many around us, who will share in the rapture of the saints because of our unwearied endeavor to win them for Jesus? May we be spared the shame of a starless crown!

SEPTEMBER 30

Who shall judge the quick [living]...at his appearing...
Preach the word.
—2 Timothy 4:1, 2

In his exhortations to Timothy, the young evangelist, Paul the aged urges him to keep the Judgment Seat in view. And that the apostle practiced what he preached is evident by his declaration, *"Henceforth there is laid up for me a crown of righteousness, which the Lord, the righteous judge, shall give me at that day"* (2 Timothy 4:8). If we claim to be the Lord's, and desire His commendation, we, too, must preach the Word, reprove, rebuke, exhort with all long-suffering and doctrine. Some of us have short tempers when it comes to those who turn away their ears from the truth. Let us not forget the *long-suffering* as we preach and teach doctrine.

FORTIETH WEEK

THE VALUE OF SOULS

OCTOBER 1

They watch for your souls.
—Hebrews 13:17

Among the admonitions of this chapter, none are so forcible as those to be found in the verse before us, which is certain a verse for pastors to ponder. My brother, if you have been set aside to minister the Word, do you constantly watch for the souls of your flock? Are you striving to guard and guide them for whom you labor, and over whom you rule? As a true spiritual adviser, do you reprove, rebuke, exhort, with all longsuffering and doctrine? At the Judgment Seat of Christ you will have to give an account of your oversight of the flock.

OCTOBER 2

His blood will I require at thine hand.
—Ezekiel 3:18

No Christian can read the solemn commission of Ezekiel and remain indifferent to the eternal destiny of souls. *"When I say to the wicked, Thou shalt surely die; and thou givest him not warning, nor speakest to warn the wicked from his wicked way, to save his life; the same wicked man shall die in his iniquity; but his blood will I require at thine hand."* Jeremiah likewise urges the believer not to have the blood of souls upon his skirts. (See Jeremiah 2:34.) It is a sobering thought that there are souls in hell who would not have been there had we be more faithful in our witness. May grace be ours to warn who come our way of the frightful eternity awaiting them they die out of Christ!

OCTOBER 3

If your soul were in my soul's stead,
I could heap up words against you.
—Job 16:4

Obadiah counseled Edom to remember the day when she stood on the other side. Once a captive and a foreigner, Edom was bidden to have sympathy for those whose distress was similar to that she herself had experienced. As a saved soul, do you remember the day when you stood on the other side? Never forget, will you, the pit from which you have been dug? And as you look around you, upon the souls of others as lost sin as you were, may yours be the yearning to lead them where you are in grace.

OCTOBER 4

The redemption of their soul is precious, and it ceaseth for ever.
—Psalm 49:8

To redeem the souls of men, God emptied heaven of the best He could find. In the sacrifice of His Son, the Father went to the limit for a prodigal race. Calvary likewise represents the value God places upon the soul of man. The gain of the whole world is reckoned poor exchange for the soul. But what is it that gives the soul its preciousness? Is it not the fact that it is of divine creation and is destined to exist forever? And, further, such was the stupendous sacrifice of Christ that the redemption of souls has ceased forever. Once for all, and for all, Christ died for sin. And now, all that a sinner can do is to accept by faith a completed redemption on his behalf.

OCTOBER 5

The soul that sinneth, it shall die.
—Ezekiel 18:20

Personal accountability is among the ethical instructions set forth by Ezekiel. Eternal death is for the sinner's own sin, and not another's. (See Jeremiah 31:29–30.) And because all have sinned, all must suffer the second death, unless they rest in the death the Savior died for sinners. It shall die! This of course, does not mean cessation of being or annihilation, seeing that the soul is indestructible. Death means separation. In physical death, it is the separation of the soul from the body. In spiritual and eternal death, it is the separation of the soul from God, now and throughout eternity. And, surely, the rescue of souls from such a death is a strong enough incentive in service.

OCTOBER 6

We...believe to the saving of the soul.
—Hebrews 10:39

Are we among the number who believes that souls can be saved? At times, we hear some degenerates referred to as being beyond redemption. But surely this is not true! No matter how hard and godless a man may be, while there is life there is hope. To confess that a gospel-hardened soul is hopeless to win is to limit the power of God. We are encouraged, then, to labor on, even for the very worst, seeing that all the time the door of mercy stands ajar, the vilest sinner may return.

OCTOBER 7

Save a soul...and...hide a multitude of sins.
—James 5:20

A strong motive in evangelism is the fact stressed by James, namely, the rescue of a soul from spiritual and eternal death and the blotting out of the past sins of such a one converted to God. And what an incentive this is! When we think on those conspicuously evil, and who, because of the multitude of their sins have a terrible eternity awaiting them, do we not find ourselves laboring unceasingly to bring these sinners to the covering blood? Solomon reminds us that *"love covereth all sins"* (Proverbs 10:12). May greater grace be ours to love the lost out of their sins and to lead them to cast a guilty past forever in the crimson stream!

FORTY-FIRST WEEK

THE NEGLECT OF SOUL

OCTOBER 8

If he shall gain the whole word, and lose his own soul? Or what
shall a man give in exchange for his soul.
—Matthew 16:26

There are two thoughts emerging from this question Jesus said to
His disciples as He pled for full, complete obedience. The first is that a
man, in gaining the whole world, may lose his soul. Spiritual aspirations
become atrophied. The fish in the Kentucky caves have eyes, but cannot
see. Being in darkness so long, they have lost the power of sight. Charles
Darwin has reminded us that his scientific studies so dominated him
the he lost the ability to appreciate music. Let us pray to be delivered
from such a tragedy in the spiritual realm. The other thought is that of
bartering the soul. Esau exchanged his birthright for a mess of pottage.
And thousands meet with delusion over such a poor exchange.

OCTOBER 9

He that sinneth against me wrongeth his own soul.
—Proverbs 8:36

When fashioned by God, the soul possesses high and hot desires.
Made for the heights, its nature has been sadly perverted by the corrupt
influences of the earth. Thus, every time a man sins against God, he
sins against that within his nature, which, at one time, was God-like.

Defiance of all God-loving desires from His creatures ever means the crucifixion of those appetites and aspirations calling out for the supreme source of satisfaction. Every sin, then, against God spells further damage for the sinner's own soul.

OCTOBER 10

No man cared for my soul.
—Psalm 142:4

The margin, quoting the Hebrew, tells us that this phrase can be translated, "No man sought after my soul." Alas, a good many unsaved people have this complaint against some of us Christians! There would be fewer sinners around if only those of us who claim to be saved had a little more care for the lost. Are you among those who seek out lost men and women? Do you know what it is to sacrifice time, put yourself about, and go out of your way, to influence a soul for Christ? Do your friends, who are strangers to grace, realize by your anxiety to win them that you truly care for their soul? May we ever share God's concern for the lost!

OCTOBER 11

I will say to my soul, Soul,
thou hast much goods laid up for many years.
—Luke 12:19

Another strong motive, making for fruitful evangelism, is the fact that we never know when God will call the lost to a just accounting. Prosperous sinners may prepare for a merry retirement, but before they commence to live on their goods, they may be snatched away to endure the misery of hell. Instead of ease, they may have everlasting torment. Solemnly, then, we must not hesitate to warn rich fools that suddenly their soul may be required of them. And, let us also tell them that they are fools indeed to provide for an earthly future, and carelessly neglect their eternal future.

OCTOBER 12

None can keep alive his own soul.
—Psalm 22:29

One evident interpretation of this sentence is that man cannot live beyond the period of divine permission. Science assures us that the span of life has been considerably lengthened. Well, life is sweet to many and they want to linger as long as they can. But when the hand of death beckons, saint and sinner, prince and pauper, alike must go. Another angle is that of divine sustenance. Only the God who created the soul can supply the true life it must have if it is to function aright. Apart from this life, the soul is dead even as it struggles to live.

OCTOBER 13

Slaves, and the souls of men.
—Revelation 18:13

The commerce of Babylon included traffic in souls. Souls were slaves. Men were bought and sold as cattle. Here, of course, is a forced slavery, and if present dictators could have their way, millions of souls would become their slaves. But there is a self-imposed slavery. Many a soul is in bondage. Sin holds the soul with a vice like grip. Are you a slave of some habit? Well, the precious blood of Christ is able to end your slavery and fashion you into a son and a servant.

OCTOBER 14

How shall we escape, if we neglect so great salvation…
—Hebrews 2:3

Negligence is the one condemning sin. At the Great White Throne sinners will be judged not because they were drunkards, gamblers or harlots, but because in the first place they neglected God's great salvation. And as *"neglect"* means to recognize and yet leave alone, is this not the peril of so many souls who, although they assent to the claims of Christ, fail to yield to them? The peril of neglect is one facing so many who constantly attend a Sunday school or church. So near to the kingdom, they yet fail to decide.

FORTY-SECOND WEEK

WISDOM

OCTOBER 15

This is your wisdom.
—Deuteronomy 4:6

In teaching a new generation the lessons of Sinai, Moses made it clear that true wisdom consisted in obedience to the revealed Word of God. *"Keep, therefore, and do them* [the statutes]; *for this is your wisdom and your understanding in the sight of the nations."* While wisdom dwells with prudence, often a man acquires fame for his prudence and sagacity, and reveals at the same time a conspicuous lack of wisdom. He betrays the most awful infatuation as to his best interests. Wisdom is the fear of God, the knowledge of God, the love of God, a right state of heart before God. Prudent, are you also wise? Wisdom springing from obedience to God *"is better than rubies"* (Proverbs 8:11; see also Job 28:28).

OCTOBER 16

Wisdom...God...giveth...liberally.
—James 1:5

Wisdom is not achieved by research but accepted by faith. Knowledge is attainable by the effort of man. There are those who know a great deal. They have attained high eminence in literature, science, or theology. Much study has brought valuable knowledge. Wisdom, however, is not gained, but given. *"God gave Solomon wisdom"* (1 Kings 4:29).

And here in James, we are reminded that the most illiterate saint, in so far as earthly knowledge is concerned, can yet become the possessor of profound wisdom. And, if true, divine wisdom can be ours for the asking. Are we not fools to remain unwise?

OCTOBER 17

Fools despise wisdom.
—Proverbs 1:7

Solomon's unique collection of Proverbs appears to revolve around two sets of individuals, namely, the wise and fools. And the book, as a whole, is an exposition of the worth of the wise and the futility of the foolish. The wise delight in wisdom from above, while fools despise such wisdom schools can never impart. Solomon links true wisdom on to the emulation of parental piety. *"My son, hear the instruction of thy father, and forsake not the law of thy mother"* (verse 8). But how many godless children there are who have outgrown the religion of their parents! Like fools, they despise the very source of power that gave them the noblest parents a child could have.

OCTOBER 18

Say unto wisdom, Thou art my sister.
—Proverbs 7:4

Some people are very proud of their relatives, especially if they are famous. On the other hand, some relations are heartlessly forgotten. Well, in *"the wisdom from above which is first pure, then peaceable, gentle, easy to be intreated, full of mercy and good fruits, without partiality, and without hypocrisy"* (James 3:17), we all have a relative we should never be ashamed to own. Many of our connections are too poor to help us in a time of need. It is a struggle for them to make ends meet. But in the wisdom of God we have a sister who is endowed with priceless riches, and who is able to bless us with untold mental and spiritual wealth.

OCTOBER 19

I, wisdom dwell with prudence and
find out knowledge of witty inventions.
—Proverbs 8:12

One of the most helpful aids to Bible study we know of gives us this enlightening comment on Solomon's eulogy of wisdom in the chapter before us. "That wisdom is more than the personification of an attribute of God, or of the will of God as best for man, but is a distinct adumbration of Christ, is sure to the devout mind. Proverbs 8:22–36 with John 1:1–3; Colossians 1:17 can refer to nothing less than the eternal Son of God." And to this agrees the declaration of Paul that God has *Christ "is made unto us wisdom, and righteousness, sanctification and redemption"* (1 Corinthians 1:30). Christ, too, is the *"hidden wisdom"* (1 Corinthians 2:7) discernible only by faith.

OCTOBER 20

Wisdom is better than strength.
—Ecclesiastes 9:16

Tucked away in this chapter is a story of a little city besieged by a powerful king, and yet delivered by the wisdom of a poor man. (See verses 14–18.) And the way this forgotten, poor, wise man saved his small city led Solomon to confess, *"Wisdom is better than strength.... Wisdom is better than weapons of war"* (Ecclesiastes 9:16, 18). We are slow to learn, however, that the arm of flesh will fail us. By the mere strength of the flesh we can never prevail over superior forces arrayed against us. And carnal weapons offer the Christian no spiritual defense whatever. Our only hope of victory is in trusting in the wisdom coming to us from above the sun.

OCTOBER 21

Wisdom...shall be the stability of thy times.
—Isaiah 33:6

Is it not somewhat of a mockery to speak of stability in a time like this? Chaos and despair afflict the earth. The bottom is falling out of things. Civilization is crumbling. Even our own personal life suffers the disrupting influences of war. And yet the prophet tells us that stability can be ours in an unstable age. With panic around, we can be at peace. Tranquility can be ours as we endure tribulation. And the secret of such stability is the wisdom of God. We may not be able to read the meaning of our tears, nor understand the anguish of earth. Faith, however, rests in the only wise God who never errs.

FORTY-THIRD WEEK

RIGHTEOUSNESS

OCTOBER 22

Made the righteousness of God in him.
—2 Corinthians 5:21

Chrysostom remarks on this passage, "The word *'righteousness'*—the unspeakable bounty of the gift, that God hath not given us only the operation of effect of His righteousness, but His very self unto us. Paul does not say that God treated Christ as a sinner, but as sin, the quality itself, in order that we might become not merely righteous men, but *'the righteousness of God in Him.'* This is the essence of the gospel. It reveals to us the grand secret of the way in which God could be just and yet pardon the sinner who puts his trust in Jesus Christ."

OCTOBER 23

My righteousness is near.
—Isaiah 51:5

"I...will ascribe righteousness to my Maker" (Job 36:3) is the absolute and essential perfection of the divine nature, and is sometimes used of God's justice. "Righteousness" is frequently employed to denote the obedience of Christ, by which all who believe are justified from all things. The word is also applied to the good works of believers, because they flow from the love to God, faith in Christ, gratitude for pardoning mercy, and because they have the divine glory for their aim and object. And it is the obligation of all saints to *"declare His righteousness unto a*

people that shall be born" (Psalm 22:31). By lip and life they must publish the gospel of righteousness from one generation to another.

OCTOBER 24

The righteousness of God which is by faith.
—Romans 3:22

What the apostle calls *"the righteousness of God"* is the state of reconciliation with God in which man is placed by the divine sentence which declares Him just. The sinner's thoughts are consequently directed from self to God, from his own efforts to His free grace; from attainment to obtainment; from the strain of working to receptivity. Righteousness, then, has a divine origin. It comes direct from God. Man, therefore, has to quit establishing his own righteousness. And, further, this divine righteousness is extended to all, and is upon all who believe. Here we have the universal destination of righteousness, *"unto all,"* and its particular application, *"upon all them that believe."*

OCTOBER 25

Made unto us...righteousness.
—1 Corinthians 1:30

John Bunyan has reminded us that the believer in Christ is now, by grace, shrouded under so complete and blessed a righteousness that the Law from Mount Sinai can find neither fault nor diminution therein. This is that which is called the righteousness of God by faith. To which we can add: "The righteousness of God is neither an attribute of God nor the changed character of the believer, but Christ Himself, who fully met in our stead and behalf every demand of the law, and who is, by the act of God, called imputation."* Righteousness, then, comes to us in a Person. The Lord is our Righteousness.

*The Old Scofield RG Study Bible, KJV, Standard Edition, Romans 3:21, study notes.

OCTOBER 26

Not by works of righteousness.
—Titus 3:5

Righteousness here represents man's futile efforts to satisfy God by His deeds. A self-established righteousness, however, is obnoxious to God. *"All our righteousnesses are as filthy rags"* (Isaiah 64:6) to a righteous God. The fine linen which is the righteousness of saints is not self-provided, but divinely bestowed. Alas, multitudes are trying hard to help God save them, and to win their way to heaven. By their morality, good deeds, and even religious activities, they feel that favor is being gained. Would that their blind eyes could be opened to discover that righteousness is a gift! And yet, while Paul scorns all works of human righteousness, he yet exhorts the truly saved to be careful to maintain good works.

OCTOBER 27

Live unto righteousness.
—1 Peter 2:24

Imputed righteousness, as we have seen, is the character and work of Christ justly reckoned to the believer, in virtue of the substitutionary work of the cross. Imparted righteousness is the working out in a believer's life in present, daily experience all the righteousness of God worked in by the Spirit. This is the implication of phrases like, *"doeth righteousness"* (Psalm 106:3)—*"fruits of righteousness"* (Philippians 1:11)—*"armour of righteousness"* (2 Corinthians 6:7)—*"awake to righteousness"* (1 Corinthians 15:34). What we are in the heavenliest is translated into holy living here on the earth, as we continually reckon ourselves to be dead to sin and alive to God.

OCTOBER 28

A preacher of righteousness...
—2 Peter 2:5

Noah was renowned as *"a preacher of righteousness,"* because of his reputation as a man of righteousness. He was righteous, not through the possession of a flawless character, but because he walked with God. As justice and equity are synonymous with righteousness, Noah knew that God was just in bringing the flood upon the world of the ungodly, and he was at one with God in such a judgment. Walking with God meant perfect agreement with Him in all things. And yet, as a faithful *"preacher of righteousness,"* and with an upright life to back up his preaching, only seven out of a vast multitude were saved.

FORTY-FOURTH WEEK

SANCTIFICATION

OCTOBER 29

Go unto the people, and sanctify them.
—Exodus 19:10

The words consecration, dedication, sanctification, and holiness all spring from one Hebrew word, and used of persons and possessions, carry the same idea, namely, set apart for God. When any of these terms are used of God, Christ, or the angels, an inward moral quality is necessarily implied. A Bible teacher remarks, "doubtless a priest or other person set apart to the service of God, whose whole will and desire went with his setting apart, experienced progressively an inner detachment from evil;* but that aspect is distinctively of the New Testament, not of the Old Testament" (See Matthew 4:5).

*The Scofield Study Bible III, NIV, page 1223.

OCTOBER 30

Sanctified in Christ Jesus.
—1 Corinthians 1:2

Sanctification, as applied to ourselves, assumes a threefold character: positional, practical and perfect. Positional, all believers are eternally set apart for God by the cross. (See Hebrews 10:9–10.) And this means that from the moment of regeneration, the Christian is counted "holy" or "*sanctified*." All believers, therefore, are saints. Practically, the believer is daily sanctified by the Holy Spirit through the holy Scriptures. Standing is translated into state. And while all believers are saints, some are more saintly in life than others. Perfectly sanctified is the future experience of believers. His holiness will be consummated when he sees the Lord Jesus Christ at His return.

OCTOBER 31

The very God of peace sanctify you wholly.
—1 Thessalonians 5:23

If our practical sanctification is "the progressive conformity of the heart and life to the will of God, and includes dying to sin and living in holiness,"* then every part of our being must bear the imprint of such a divine work. To use a new translation of this Pauline exhortation, we must be "consecrated through and through. Spirit, soul, and body, may you be kept without break or blame until the arrival of our Lord Jesus Christ." Surely, we could not wish for a better definition of sanctification than this without break or blame until Christ's arrival! And let us not forget that the God who calls us to sanctification is the One who supplies it.

*Barr, John, *Complete Index and Concise Dictionary of the Holy Bible.*

NOVEMBER 1

This is the will of God, even your sanctification.
—1 Thessalonians 4:3

Holiness, then, is the *will* as well as the *work* of God. And what He wills He is able to work if only we will let Him. But why is our sanctification a part of the divine will? Well, first of all, God Himself is holy and therefore His children must know how to walk and please Him. Our walk must not be alien to His will. And then, holiness is imperative for progress in the Christian life. If one is beset by the lusts of the flesh, how can they approximate the likeness of God? Further, by separation from all uncleanness, the saint recommends the gospel of sanctification to multitudes who find themselves miserably defeated by the forces of the old nature.

NOVEMBER 2

Sanctification of the Spirit.
—2 Thessalonians 2:13

Holiness is a divine work the Holy Spirit is directly responsible for. It is He Who, from the moment of our regeneration, endeavors to make our character conform to our calling. Understanding the mind of God concerning sin and self, the spirit can develop saintliness according to divine requirements. It is also interesting to note Paul's connection between sanctification and orthodoxy. Salvation—sanctification--soundness, were co-related in the apostle's thinking. Sanctification is impossible if there is not the basis of salvation, and any one denying the cardinal truths of the faith has no claim to the work of the Spirit in sanctification. We are sanctified through the truth.

NOVEMBER 3

Clean…stronger and stronger.
—Job 17:9; Proverbs 4:18

Sanctification can never be fully realized unless it is an unhindered progressive experience. In fact, it is a crisis leading to a process, brought to a more blessed understanding of the requirements and resources of God's holy will, so often saints come to the place of completer dedication to that will. This is the crisis. But as the light shines more and more, with clearer, fuller light focused upon our daily walk, unconscious impediments to holiness become conscious, and are immediately yielded to the blood. This is the process.

NOVEMBER 4

Sanctify them...I sanctify myself.
—John 17:17–19

When our Lord spoke of sanctifying Himself, He simply had in mind the setting of Himself apart for God's service. As the sinless One, He had nothing unclean to lay aside. The desire to please God was the undying passion of His life. Therefore, all else had to be subservient to His dedication. And in this He has left us an example that we should follow in His steps. There is also here, the emphasis on the channel of sanctification, namely, through the truth.

FORTY-FIFTH WEEK

REDEMPTION

NOVEMBER 5

The redemption that is in Christ Jesus.
—Romans 3:24

The central idea of the word *redeem* is to buy back what was sold, pledged, forfeited, or to deliver by paying a price. The full truth of redemption is indicated by the three words translated into such a general term. The first term suggests a purchase in a market. Before us is a slave market with those the Lord came to redeem sold under sin, and under sentence of death. The purchase price for enslaved souls is the blood of the Redeemer, Who willingly dies in their stead. The next word carries with it the idea of being brought out of the market. The purchase is so complete that those bought out with a price are never again to be exposed to sale. Then we have a third word meaning to liberate, to set free by paying a price. The slave's redemption is by sacrifice. Christ paid the price, and the Spirit makes deliverance an actual experience.

NOVEMBER 6

Not redeemed with corruptible things.
—1 Peter 1:18

Under the Mosaic economy the redemption of anything was only possible by the surrender of coined gold or silver. By the *"vain conversation"* we are to understand the traditions of the elders our Lord

175

condemned, and which Paul was brought up in, and was zealous of preserving before he found Christ. Precious as gold and silver is, being among the corruptible things; mere metal could never redeem a soul destined to live forever. Something infinitely more precious was necessary, and in the precious blood of Christ we have the cost to God of the soul's emancipation from sin's enslavement. (See Isaiah 52:3.) And what a delusion it is for men to try and buy their peace with God.

NOVEMBER 7

The right of redemption is thine to buy it.
—Jeremiah 32:7

The Old Testament supplies us with some examples of redemption by ransom or price. There is the priceless story of Ruth and Boaz, her kinsman-redeemer. And Jeremiah supplies us with the illustration of the redemption of Hanameel's field. Without doubt the redeemer ordained by Moses prefigured Jesus as the Redeemer of the world. As one writer has expressed it, "The human race wholly lost, sentenced to death, and excluded from the inheritance of spiritual and eternal life no mere created being could redeem. By the dominion of sin over them, they were captives of Satan, and justly doomed to eternal woe. They had no kinsman to vindicate their cause, to interpose for them by power or price. The glory of the gospel is that Christ came, and by giving Himself as a ransom, provided a perfect redemption."

NOVEMBER 8

Christ...is made unto us...redemption.
—1 Corinthians 1:30

One of the marvelous things about the manifold provisions of God is that they all seem to head up in Christ. All are in and through the Son. Too often we think of gifts apart from the Giver. It is sadly possible to devote columns to a study of the various aspects of the substitutionary work of the cross, and lose sight of the One Who really died as the Substitute. There is a tendency in theological circles to smooth away all concrete Christian dogmas into a vague theism or a vaguer pantheism, and to flatten out the firm line of Christian ethics into a pious sentiment.

NOVEMBER 9

Redeeming the time…
—Colossians 4:5

The redemptive work of Christ has a claim upon all we are and have. Therefore when we say we are redeemed we ought to recognize the necessity of having the shadow of the cross fall upon every part of our life. Here, Paul brings our moments and days into the realm of redemption. His injunction can be translated "Make the very most of your time," or "Buy up the opportunity." And, truly, time is in the market, and must be bought. Satan would have us buy time and waste it. But it is God's purpose that each flying minute might contribute to His glory and achieve something lasting by way of benefit for the souls of men.

NOVEMBER 10

Their Redeemer is strong.
—Jeremiah 50:34

Solomon and Isaiah join with Jeremiah in extolling the might of our Redeemer. (See Proverbs 23:11; Isaiah 49:26.) And strong He must have been when at Calvary, He laid hold of the dark forces of hell and spoiled them of their power. By His power He conquered Satan, the slave owner, and redeemed the sin-bound from the curse and the grave. And, His resurrection added to His might. His is the strength of a glorious Conqueror. This means that He can now save the worst, and deliver the most abandoned sinner from his bondage and despair. Mighty as Christ is, He can stoop to the sinner's weakness and empower him to live above sin.

NOVEMBER 11

With him is plenteous redemption.
—Psalm 130:7

With His own blood, Jesus obtained an eternal redemption for us, and being eternal, it is plenteous. Millions have participated in a blood-bought salvation, and yet there is provision for millions more. How stupendous and far-reaching was the work of the cross! We think of China with its four hundred million, India with its well-nigh three hundred twenty million, America with its one hundred thirty-five million*, and to realize that everyone among the myriads of earth can experience the cleansing efficacy of the blood and become children of God if they are only willing to repent and believe. All souls have been redeemed but only few in comparison have appropriated their redemption.

* Editor's note: population figures updated at the time of publication are China (1.3 billion), India (1.2 billion), and the U.S. (318 million).

FORTY-SIXTH WEEK

HIS BEAUTIFUL HANDS

NOVEMBER 12

My times are in thy hand.
—Psalm 31:15

Palmists are those who profess to have the power of reading your hands and relating them to your history, thus predicting your future fortunes or misfortunes. It is to be hoped that as Christian you never patronize palmistry, seeing that your times are not in your hands, but in *His*. My times! Yes, all time whether they be pleasant or painful, glad or sad, good or grievous—all times and all the time is in His mighty hands. And the means that nothing can reach a believer apart from divine permission. His hands not only protect and provide, but hold check those hostile forces seeking the destruction of His own.

NOVEMBER 13

Behold my hands…
—John 20:27

We are apt to forget that the hands of Jesus were human hands. They were the hands of a carpenter, and bore the insignia of His handiwork. Tolstoy represents the ideal czar as one who keeps an open house and well-laden table for all comers. But the guests had to face one condition: Each had to show two hands before sitting down at the feast. Those with hands hard and rough with honest work were welcomed to the best the table afforded, while those with soft, white hands had to be content with crusts and crumbs.

NOVEMBER 14

Mighty works are wrought by his hands.
—Mark 6:2

Gertrude Bell wrote of Lawrence of Arabia,—"everything that he touches, flowers." And, surely, such is descriptive of the impact of Christ's gripping and vivifying fingers. He touched nothing into which He did not bring a new atmosphere of blessing and holiness. A study of the gospels reveals that the miraculous ministry of Jesus was made possible through the touch of His hands. Oliver Goldsmith's monument in Westminster Abbey bears the inscription. "He touched nothing which he did not adorn." Such a beautiful sentiment might have been written of the touch of Christ, for through His hands life, health, strength, speech and sight were imparted to needy souls.

NOVEMBER 15

What are these wounds in thine hands?
—Zechariah 13:6

Because of what Thomas saw in the outstretched hands of Jesus, he willingly confessed the deity and sovereignty of the One whose resurrection he had just doubted. The religious leaders were gratified as they looked up at the hands of Jesus made fast to a cross with Roman nails. Evidently they had triumphed over those bountiful, beautiful hands. At last, they were bloodstained hands. But nail-pierced, those hands were to have greater power. As the result of His scars, Jesus wields greater power. We can read the story of our salvation in His torn hands.

NOVEMBER 16

Pluck them out of my hand.
—John 10:28

The hands of Jesus, then, are the hands of a Keeper as well as the hands of a Savior. Have you noticed the double grip here? *"Out of my hand...out of my Father's hand"* (John 10:28–29). Thus the believer is doubly secure. If our name is graven upon the hand of Christ, and also upon the hand of the Father, no one will ever be able to erase it. History relates that Wellington commanded an officer to undertake a perilous task. For a moment he seemed to shrink from such hazardous service, but facing the Iron Duke he said, "Let me before I go have one grip of your all-conquering hand, and then I can do it." And, with the inspiration of Christ's hand-grip, we can do and dare anything He commands.

NOVEMBER 17

He lifted up his hands, and blessed them.
—Luke 24:50

In this last action of the pierced hands we have symbolized Christ's present intercessory ministry as the great High Priest. Uplifted in priestly blessing as He leaves His own, they have remained uplifted. *"He ever liveth to make intercession for us"* (Hebrews 7:25).

Israel prevailed over her enemies all the time the hands of Moses remained uplifted. And the church of Christ cannot fail, seeing she has the ceaseless prayer of Jesus surrounding her. Are we emulating this intercessory ministry? Men are to pray everywhere lifting up holy hands. Rejected as saving, praying hands, they are to be seen as condemning hands. And what a fearful thing it will be to fall into the hands of a living God!

NOVEMBER 18

The hands of the living God.
—Hebrews 10:31

What a solemn truth the writer is here emphasizing! The hands that are presently extended in grace, are to be stretched out in judgment. And, truly, it will be a fearful thing to fall into the hands of such a just God! May you here gaze upon the nail-pierced hands as they take the Book of Life and proclaim the eternal woe of those whose names are not inscribed therein!

FORTY-SEVENTH WEEK

HIS WONDERFUL FACE

NOVEMBER 19

The face of the Lord is against them that do evil.
—Psalm 34:16

The face is the mirror of the soul. It is ever an index of the mind. The various passions such as love, hatred, joy, sorrow, pleasure, confidence and despair are indicated by the aspect of the countenance. Often "*face*" denotes person or character. The face of a man is used of the man himself. (See Genesis 48:11.) "*Face*" as applied to the Lord implies different aspects of His nature. In the passage introducing this daily portion, the anger of the Lord is implied. Sinners seem to forget that God is angry with them and angry with them every moment they remain in sin. The saved, however, have the blessed face of the Savior toward them. Grace brings a sinner and the Savior face to face.

NOVEMBER 20

Look upon the face of thine anointed.
—Psalm 84:9

All are sinners by birth and becoming sinners by practice. The infinite God will only extend mercy and favor to such through His beloved Son. Thus, those who are saved are viewed as being in Christ. As the Anointed, He has the smile of His Father's face. Calvary satisfied the justice of God, and likewise revealed His love. And now, God can regard the sinner in men through the mediation of Christ, the anointed Savior. It also blessed to realize that being saved, we are known as "anointed ones" and that being the Lord's, we have the smiling of His face. Ere long we shall see Him face to face.

NOVEMBER 21

Then did they spit in his face.
—Matthew 26:67

The marvel of the Master is that although He knew that His face, reflecting as it did the glory of God, was to suffer the coarse, brutal indignities of godless men, yet steadfastly set that face to go to Jerusalem in order to die for men. Isaiah tells us that Christ's *"visage was…marred more than any man,"* (Isaiah 52:14), a phrase which when literally rendered, implies that His lovely face was brutally battered almost beyond recognition. Ah, the world has a strange way of rewarding holiness! The next time you have to endure a little reproach for Christ's sake, say to yourself, especially if tempted to self-pity, "Well, so far no one has spit on my face."

NOVEMBER 22

From whose face the earth and the heaven fled away.
—Revelation 20:11

Demons and men will tremble at the look on the face of the Judge as He sits on the Great White Throne. Doomed souls will cry to be hid from the Lord's stern countenance. In His humiliation, He silently endured the spittle and the blows of His rejecters, but that face of shame is yet to be the face of sovereignty. One look of that serene face, wreathed with the determination of righteous judgment, will be sufficient to chase everything material into oblivion. May you be spared from seeing that face, the look of which the lost in the lake of fire will never forget!

NOVEMBER 23

They shall see his face.
—Revelation 22:4

In John's description of the celestial city, nothing ravishes the soul of the believer like the thought that he is to gaze eternally upon the beautiful face of the glorified Christ. Do you live in anticipation of the thrill when, for the first time, you will see Jesus? When, with rapture we behold Him, depend upon it, we will be speechless! The young man Absalom dwelt two full years in Jerusalem, and saw not the king's face. Near the king, yet not allowed to see his face? Praise God, this will never be the experience of any born-again one! The moment the eyes of a saved person close upon earth, immediately he enters heaven, there to see the King in all His beauty.

NOVEMBER 24

The glory of God in the face of Jesus Christ.
—2 Corinthians 4:6

Jesus had a glory face. Have you? Our Lord bore His great commission in His look. Coming as the culmination of the revelation of the Father, the Master's very countenance carried an unearthly serenity. Without assumption He could confess, *"He that hath seen me hath seen the Father"* (John 14:9). Can we say that our features reflect the presence of the Lord within? The murderers of Stephen saw his face as it had been the face of an angel. Do we carry an unconscious angelic look?

NOVEMBER 25

I set my face like a flint.
—Isaiah 50:7

Without doubt the prophet, inspired by the Holy Spirit, displays the humiliation Christ was to suffer. And as He came among men, He knew what awaited Him. Did He shrink from the cross He was sent to die upon? A thousand times, No! Satan tried to kill Him before Calvary, but Jesus walked with a resolute step to that hill, lone and gray, where He ultimately died as a Victor. And His noble face, so determined looking, declared His firm purpose. He steadfastly set his face to go to Jerusalem. His face was as though he would go to Jerusalem. What dogged perseverance characterized His features! One glance at that face convinced His foes that Christ meant to endure the cross and despise all shame.

FORTY-EIGHTH WEEK

HIS MANY CROWNS

NOVEMBER 26

On his head were many crowns.
—Revelation 19:12

As the representative of the Father, the Lord Jesus Christ holds sway in every realm. Delegated authority is His to add in a sovereign capacity. (See John 5:22–27.) The many diadems on His brow may be thus regarded: The crown of creation—the crown of providence—the crown of history—the crown of redemption—the crown of universal dominion—the crown of everlasting glory. The question is: Does the crown of your implicit obedience repose upon His kingly head?

NOVEMBER 27

Thou crownedst him with glory and honour.
—Hebrews 2:7

Crowns are figuratively used of honor, splendor and dignity. That which adds glory and prestige to a person is denominated a crown. (See Lamentations 5:16; Isaiah 28:5.) Military crowns were conferred upon victorious generals for valor. One of the crowns David wore was valued at about thirty thousand dollars. (See 2 Samuel 12:30.) But what are the costly crowns of earth in comparison with Christ's crown of glory? As yet, He has not received His diadem, as World-Emperor. His crowning day, however, is not far distant. We see not yet all things put under

Him. In heaven, He is fully recognized as being crowned. Perpetual adoration is offered by the glorified to the Lamb upon His throne.

NOVEMBER 28

They platted a crown of thorns.
—Matthew 27:29

The thorns in question were small, sharp spines, well adapted to give pain. And the crown was produced by contempt, its design being cruelty. Twined around Christ's head, it assimilated Him to a crowned king, and at the same time was an indication of scorn and insult. What a terrible crown for such a noble head, piercing thorns for the brow of the King Eternal! Thorns, however, are the evidence of the curse pronounced upon the earth as the result of man's sin. (See Genesis 3:17–18.) And seeing that Jesus came to bear the curse, His thorn-crowned brow revealed Him as the curse-bearer. (See Galatians 3:13.)

NOVEMBER 29

The LORD of hosts be for a crown of glory.
—Isaiah 28:5

Strikingly expressive of all the Lord will yet accomplish for the residue of His people, the Jews, the crown of glory here is in contrast to the "crown of pride" the drunkards of Ephraim were to lose. (See verse 3.) While, of course, we are not to understand the wearing of an actual crown, what such symbolizes is applicable both to the Lord and Ephraim. The implication is that all false crowns, and all temporary crowns are to pass, but Christ's glory and sovereignty are eternal. And during the reign of Christ, the Jews as well as the world are to behold His diadem of beauty. We speak of a head being uneasy that wears a crown, and some crowned heads are having anxious days. But when He is crowned Monarch of the world, Christ will be dauntless.

NOVEMBER 30

On his head a golden crown.
—Revelation 14:14

If what we have in the immediate narrative is a vision of Armageddon, then we can understand the import of this crown of gold upon the head of the Son of Man. From time immemorial crowns of gold have represented monarchy. Kings and crowns go together. At Armageddon, crowned and uncrowned rulers are to be gathered against the Lord and His anointed. It is therefore fitting that as Christ returns as the King of Kings, in order to fashion the kingdoms of the world into His own world kingdom that He should appear with the insignia of His royalty and sovereignty. A diadem of surpassing worth will sit upon the mighty Victor's brow.

DECEMBER 1

…the holy crown….
—Leviticus 8:9

Head ornaments in the East were deemed a mark of dignity and honor. They were used to distinguish the chief rulers, civil and ecclesiastic. It was thus that the Jewish high priest was known by a diadem, tied with a ribbon of hyacinth color. Set apart for holy work, Aaron had a crown corresponding to his life and labors. The Psalmist reminds us of those who, although anointed of God, profaning their crown by casting it to the ground. But Christ, as the great High Priest, has a crown of holiness that has never been profaned. Holy, harmless and undefiled, He could ask, *"Which of you convinceth me of sin?"* (John 8:46).

DECEMBER 2

And cast their crowns before the throne.
—Revelation 4:10

While it is not within the limit of the day's portion to enumerate the many crowns offered the believer, yet the fact remains that rewards in the shape of crowns are to be ours for faithful service. But what are we going to do with these diadems? Strut around wearing them? Yes, of course, we love to sing, "I shall wear a golden crown when I get home."* Seeing the majestic Savior, however, we are to cast our crowns before His throne, saying "Thou art worthy, O Lord, to receive glory and honour and power" (Revelation 4:11). Loyalty to Him on earth brings us glory, honor and power as we commence to reign with Him. But as He made the crowns possible, they are gladly surrendered. Rewards become gifts to the King.

*C. Austin Miles, "I Shall Wear a Golden Crown."

FORTY-NINTH WEEK

HIS GLORIOUS APPAREL

DECEMBER 3

...glorious in his apparel...
—Isaiah 63:1

We sometimes hear it said that "clothes make the man." And it is surprising how clothes can alter the looks of a person. Character, too, is expressed in what we like to wear. Has it ever occurred to you to examine our Lord's wardrobe? What He wore, and wears, indicates His varied ministry. And it does not matter how we find Him clothed, He is ever glorious in whatever apparel He wears. He did not require any clothes to make Him. His intrinsic character persists in spite of the garments He cast around Him.

DECEMBER 4

He...was clad with zeal as a cloak.
—Isaiah 59:17

Zeal is a fervent passion or earnest desire for anything, but is only commendable when it is enlightened and pure. When a person has zeal, without knowledge, then it produces bigotry and prejudice and inevitably leads to fury and persecution. The zeal Christ manifested was transparent. It consisted of a high and holy regard for God's honor and also His own. The zeal of God's house consumed Him. (See Psalm 69:9.) His passion to please the Father was undying. He is likewise zealous regarding the welfare of His own. Thus, in His service for God and His people, Christ was never without His cloak of zeal.

DECEMBER 5

Naked, and ye clothed me.
—Matthew 25:36

While the narrative is taken up with the judgment of the living nations at the return of the Lord in glory, and the statement of feeding and clothing Him must be interpreted in connection with such, we are yet warranted in deducing a personal supplication. Would you like to have the privilege of clothing Christ? Why, if He asked you for an actual garment, you would hasten to buy the very best money could secure! Well, have you a suit or dress to spare? If so, look around for a brother or sister in Christ whose penury makes new or good clothes impossible, and send them what you do not need.

DECEMBER 6

A woman…touched the hem of his garment.
—Matthew 9:20

Under the Mosaic economy, every Jew had to wear a ribbon of blue upon his garment. Being a rich and magnificent color and emblematic of purity and heavenly graces, blue reminded Israel that as God's people they had to be heavenly in obedience and character and separate from earthly ambitions and desires. The Pharisees enlarged upon this requirement as a sign of unusual sanctity. It is thought that our Lord, as a Jew, wore the ribbon of blue, and that it was this hem the woman with an issue of blood touched. This garment proclaims Jesus to be the Healer Divine. And His seamless robe is ever beside the bed of pain.

DECEMBER 7

All thy garments smell of myrrh, and aloes, and cassia.
—Psalm 45:8

The Easterners were fond of perfuming their clothes, especially upon festive occasions. And among ourselves it is a common practice to scent our clothing. Christ's garments, however, did not carry any mere external fragrance. Coming out of the ivory palaces, He carried with Him the aroma of heaven. And such could not be hid!

My Lord has garments so wondrous fine,
And myrrh their texture fills;
Its fragrance reached to this heart of mine,
With joy my being fills.
(Lyric from "My Lord Has Garments So Wondrous Fine")

DECEMBER 8

The linen clothes...the napkin...wrapped together.
—John 20:5, 7

Fine white linen symbolizes purity, innocence and dignity. Thus in the linen clothes we have the holiness of the One who had worn them. What Christ's risen form had as a covering we are not told! It is clearly evident, however, that the clothes securely wrapped around His dead body, along with the cloth bound around His face, were left behind in the grave. And His withdrawal from such a shroud declared Him to be the Resurrection and the Life. It is interesting to note that the napkin was by itself, neatly folded. Folded! Yes, ere long we shall fold up all our handkerchiefs, for the empty tomb is a pledge that all our tears are to be wiped away.

DECEMBER 9

His…coat was without seam.
—John 19:23

The Jews wore two principal garments; the interior was known as a coat, or tunic; the exterior, which was worn over the coat, as a mantle or cloak. The coat was woven like a stocking in its proper shape and size, without any seam. Such were probably the fine linen of woven work Aaron and his sons wore, and which was the garment of Christ's the soldiers gambled over. Considered of great value, the gamblers kept it whole. Without seam! How true of His life, which was one perfect whole!

FIFTIETH WEEK

THE COMPANY WE KEEP

DECEMBER 10

They that feared the LORD...
—Malachi 3:16

Truly there is nothing comparable to the fellowship of the saints! Drawn to the Lord we find ourselves drawn to all those who love Him and His Word. Alas, we do not cultivate Christian conversation as we ought! We often meet our brothers and sisters in Christ but fail to speak of our blessed Lord as we should. May grace be ours, as we contact our fellow pilgrims, to be so full of what the Lord has done, that our talk will indicate our gratitude for His goodness!

DECEMBER 11

But they, supposing him to have been in the company,
went a day's journey.
—Luke 2:44

How many there are who suppose that they have Christ in the heart but who are yet destitute of His presence! They depend upon a mere supposition. Joseph and Mary supposed Jesus was with them and journeyed on for a whole day before they made the fatal discovery that He was not around. And it may be that you are taking it for granted that Jesus is in your company, because you are somewhat religious, and go to a church where others gather to worship His name. Have you definitely received Him as your personal Savior? At some time or another was there the definite committal of your life to Him? Then, He is with you, and His presence is a blessed reality. If you are not His, then He is not in your company and you are certainly not in His company.

DECEMBER 12

The countenance of his friend.
—Proverbs 27:17

In the expressive metaphor of iron sharpening iron, Solomon is emphasizing the exhilarating effect of wholesome conversation as saint meets saint. And what a tonic it is to come across a Christian whose words are so cheerful and encouraging! If dull and disconsolate because of trial and adversity, we find our burdens lightened as a friend, whose happy face and comforting talk crosses our path and bids us take fresh courage. Are you active in this necessary ministry of sharpening countenances? There are multitudes of sad faces belonging to those whose loads are heavy. Do not fail them as you meet them! Ask God for the words you need to chase the shadows away from the face of the sorrowful. Let us endeavor to make every life the better for having met us on the rugged pilgrimage towards heaven!

DECEMBER 13

A companion of fools shall be destroyed.
—Proverbs 13:20

Solomon gives us a double picture in the proverb he cites. Walking with the wise, we become wise: walking with fools we become like them, all of which means that our companionship influences character. The company we keep is not only an index of our spiritual life, but has a decided influence upon our thought and action. And as companions of those we are able to choose for ourselves, are we not acting against our own mental and moral development when we fail to form friendship with those who fear God and who ever entertain high and noble thoughts of life? If you have a companionship disastrous to your spiritual welfare, then sever it at once.

DECEMBER 14

Blessed is the man that walketh not in the counsel of the ungodly.
—Psalm 1:1

The perilous progress of sin is traced by the psalmist in a threefold gradation: walk, stand, and sit. Here we have devolution rather than evolution. And another trial expresses greater progress in sin: ungodly, sinners, scoffers. Our responsibility is to guard the first step. And how blessed we are if we keep away from the ungodly. Some there are who try to go as near to the fire as possible without being burnt. Our safety, however, consists in being lost in God and in His Law.

DECEMBER 15

Come out...and be ye separate.
—2 Corinthians 6:17

In Paul's appeal to the Corinthians to be separated he makes it clear that they are to be negatively separated from all whose ways are alien to the mind of God; and, positively, separated unto God for the fulfill-ment of His will. Possibly your spiritual life is somewhat low because of wrong and forbidden associations. The company you keep is carnal in outlook, and consequently your desire for the deeper things is thwarted. It may be that if you determine to quit certain company that you will instantly experience a liberation of divine power in and through your life? Unequally yoked together with unbelievers in clubs, lodges, societ-ies, business and pleasure is often a serious handicap to one's spiritual progress.

DECEMBER 16

Being let go, they went to their own company.
—Acts 4:23

Peter and John could not be at home in the presence of those who forbad them to speak or teach in the name of Jesus. As soon as they got away from the rulers, elders and scribes who had no sympathy with their message of a crucified risen Savior, they bounded home to those who were like-minded as themselves. "Birds of a feather flock together." What kind of company do you seek once you are free from business cares and responsibilities? With the world around you all day, do you run away when time is your own to those who love the Lord?

FIFTY-FIRST WEEK

GODLY CONTENTMENT

DECEMBER 17

His brethren were content.
—Genesis 37:27

The contentment experienced by the cruel brothers of Joseph meant that his young life was spared a horrible end. Judah's plea to sell Joseph rather than slay him satisfied a jealous feeling. But such contentment as Joseph's brothers experienced was false and fickle. The cries and moans of the lad as in anguish of soul he pleaded for mercy were ever in their ears and haunted them through the days. Jealousy, cruelty, deceit, can never produce true abiding contentment. When spite has been meted out upon someone we dislike, vengeance may produce a feeling of satisfaction. Revenge is sweet, we say. It is likewise satanic.

DECEMBER 18

Would to God we had been content.
—Joshua 7:7

Constant discontent on the part of the Israelites earned the displeasure and judgment of God. How the people murmured! The book of Numbers finds them complaining in eight different ways as they journeyed through the wilderness. Joshua, humiliated by his defeat of Ai, could not understand how God had allowed his men to be driven from the gates of the city. It would have been better for the chosen of the Lord to have remained in Egypt and been content with their bondage than to have a victorious journey crowned with such conquest at the hands of those they had come to conquer. Sin, however, was in the camp. Therefore, the wail of Joshua regarding contentment was unjustified. There is such a thing as a holy discontent. It was this that prompted the people to bear the bondage of Egypt.

DECEMBER 19

He will not regard any ransom; neither will he rest content.
—Proverbs 6:35

The rage of a jealous-minded man can never be appeased. His vengeful spirit cannot be satisfied. Gifts expressing goodwill fail to pacify him. The passion for revenge can never be bought off. Have you ever noticed that there is nothing calm, serene, or tranquil about a jealous person? As true contentment is related to the mind, it is necessary to guard oneself against disturbing elements. Wrong feelings toward another agitate our thought-life.

DECEMBER 20

Pilate, willing to content the people…delivered Jesus.
—Mark 15:15

Had Pilate acted the other way and released Jesus, he would have gone down in history as a courageous man! He was guilty, however, of placing position before conscience. His better nature as well as his better half, told him that Christ was innocent, but the crowd clamored for His death so what could he do? Many a preacher has succumbed to Pilate's temptation. Willing to content the worldly minded around them, they have soft pedaled. Accommodating themselves to popular demand, preachers, anxious to retain a good position, have been guilty of silence in the sterner side of the gospel. But one called of God must be willing to content the heart of the One sending him, no matter what discontent or displeasure his faithful ministry may produce.

DECEMBER 21

I have learned...to be content.
—Philippians 4:11

The autobiography of Paul proves that he practiced what he preached. Often his state was a very precarious one, yet he was never guilty of grumbling. Writing to Timothy he urged him to be content if all that he had was food and raiment. Yet there were times when Paul lacked an adequate supply of food and raiment. Christ told those around him to be content with their wages. Contentment is not an easy lesson to learn in the school of life. Do you not find yourself rebuked by the apostle's confession? In whatsoever state! It is easy to be content when the state is affluent and pleasing. But when our state is characterized by need and trial then grace alone can save us from discontentment.

DECEMBER 22

Be content with such things as ye have.
—Hebrews 13:5

To go to one in straitened circumstances and say, "Be content with what you have," when we know how little they do have would only mock their feelings, unless we know how to point them to Him whose presence and provision are ever granted to those who trust Him. (See Proverbs 15:16.) Are you content with what you have, knowing that if the Lord desires you to possess what is presently withheld, that in His own way and time He will make up to you what may be lacking? If we have Christ, let us leave our cares with Him.

DECEMBER 23

Godliness with contentment is great gain.
—1 Timothy 6:6

Contentment, then, is not self-manufactured. It springs from godliness. It is not a question of trying to be content under all circumstances, but the willingness to abide in the will of God that produces the coveted grace we have considered this week. And, truly, godly contentment is great gain. Think of what we ourselves gain! In a discontented world we exhibit poise, confidence, and tranquility commendable to our Christian profession. Contentment in a believer is likewise beneficial to those around. Tempted to fuss, fume and worry, our God-begotten calm even when we do suffer, brings those whose minds are like a troubled sea, to a new understanding of the marvelous grace of our God. Then, He too, becomes a gainer by our contented spirit.

FIFTY-SECOND WEEK

THE END

DECEMBER 24

Thy years shall have no end.
—Psalm 102:27

As we have come to the end of the year it is but fitting to consider a few Bible "ends." In December we think of the last things. Another year has almost run its course like the thousands of years before it. And our own years will end either in death or our translation at the return of Christ. But here is One whose years have no end. There are no wrinkles on God's brow. He is never weary with age. Death can never terminate His existence. He is changeless, timeless, deathless.

DECEMBER 25

Better is the end of a thing.
—Ecclesiastes 7:8

How true a sentiment this is, especially as we think of the sorrows and trials the closing year has witnessed! Looking back we marvel at the way we stood up against such grievous adversities, and we find ourselves saying, "Thank God, the year is ending! I will not have to travel that way again." The end of a good life is likewise better than the beginning thereof. Starting out upon the voyage we have all of its storms to face, but nearing port, we breathe a sigh of relief. Alas, every end is not better than the beginning! Life opens with fair promise, but its *"end is bitter as wormwood"* (Proverbs 5:4). If the fast dying year has witnessed many a failure, and you are conscious of transgression, a frank, honest confession will cause the end of the year to be better than some of its opening months.

DECEMBER 26

At the time appointed the end shall be.
—Daniel 8:19

Daniel has the same prophetic end in view when he prayed, "*O my Lord, what shall be the end of these things?*" (Daniel 12:8), to which can be added the words of the Master, "*The end is not yet*" (Matthew 24:6). The thought we want to emphasize is that any end is of divine appointment. Whether it be the end of a period or a person, God determines the termination thereof. And God is never before the time, neither is He late. At the time He decrees, His hand is seen. Often we seek to hasten the end of some things. We grow impatient and try to push the hands of the clock forward. But surely if God can wait until the opportune moment arrives for Him to fulfill His will we ought to be able to manifest patience.

DECEMBER 27

The end of all things is at hand.
—1 Peter 4:7

It must be evident to the most casual observer that the chaos on every hand indicates a climax. Something is about to happen. Those of us who accept the more sure word of prophecy believe that Someone is coming. And when Christ does appear, our Christian witness will be at an end. Some of our many privileges like prayer and testimony and giving will reach their end. "Soon will the season of rescue be o'er."* Our opportunities are becoming fewer as the days roll by. May we use the rest of time as unto the Lord! Because we may be nearer heaven than we think, may we find ourselves more deeply exercised about our own holiness, and also the salvation of never dying souls at home and abroad.

*Edwin S. Ufford, "Throw Out the Lifeline."

DECEMBER 28

Our end is come.
—Lamentations 4:18

The Lamentations of Jeremiah form a sorrowful book. Everywhere love and sorrow meet. In the portion before us souls cruelly persecuted await a terrible end. Hunted by those who were swifter than eagles, the people who are represented as watching in vain for help know that a brutal death is near. Can you not read pathos in the lament, *"Our end is come"*? What an end it must have been! How will you fare when your end is come? John Wesley declared that his preachers always died well. If we are to die well we must live well. Grace to die will be given at the last hour. What we sadly need is grace to live. God will care for the last weary mile of the road if life's daily pilgrimage has been pleasing to Him.

DECEMBER 29

The end of that man is peace.
—Psalm 37:37

In another connection (see 1 Kings 8:61), a Bible teacher reminds us that "the word 'perfect' implies wholeheartedness for God, single mindedness, sincerity—not sinless perfection." Well if such traits are ours we can expect a happy landing on eternity's broad fields. Blessed are the dead who die in the Lord. Voltaire, the French skeptic, never had a peaceful end. His nurse testified to the horrible hours he spent on his death bed. How different was the end of D. L. Moody, who looked upon his death as a coronation day. At peace with God, the famous evangelist had a peaceful end.

DECEMBER 30

I am...the end.
—Revelation 21:6

Jesus is indeed "our life, our way, our end."* He is the beginning and the end. Yes, and all in between. There is nothing before or beyond Him. As the End, Christ is to be the great finale. He will be the End of revelation, history, and time. And of His reign there is to be no end. What is to be the end of all things? To our delight Christ steps forward and affirms that He is the End. In Himself He is the focal point, the goal of divine purposes, and human wishes. And when ultimately He winds up everything, the universe will be transformed, Satan forever consigned to the lake of fire, the saints perfect and glorified, and God at last satisfied. And as the End, Christ will be just in both His commendations and condemnations. Is this Savior yours? Has He given you a new beginning? Then know that He will perfect what His love began.

*John Newton, "How Sweet the Name of Jesus Sounds."

DECEMBER 31

The power of an endless life.
—Hebrews 7:16

Here we are at the year's end. Near to midnight many saints will gather at watch night services to spend the closing moments in penitence and prayer. The past will be reviewed and cleansing sought for the failure marking the way. But although we recognize the passing of the old year, and the dawning of a new, the Lord offers the sinning sons and daughters of Adam's race the power of an endless life. What blessed continuance! God grant that when my December reaches the end of its thirty-first day, the new sun will rise bringing the New Year of unending bliss! Thus, as we part company with another year and watch its death, let us praise God for the promise of a life in which our years will know no end.

I lay in dust life's glory dead,
And from the ground there blossoms red
Life that shall endless be.
(lyric from "O Love That Wilt Not Let Me Go")

Welcome to Our House!

We Have a Special Gift for You ...

It is our privilege and pleasure to share in your love of Christian classics by publishing books that enrich your life and encourage your faith.

To show our appreciation, we invite you to sign up to receive a specially selected **Reader Appreciation Gift**, with our compliments. Just go to the Web address at the bottom of this page.

God bless you as you seek a deeper walk with Him!

WE HAVE A GIFT FOR YOU

whpub.me/classicthx

WHITAKER
HOUSE